Ce

D0812558

WINTER
IN
CASTILLE

CE

HONOR TRACY

WINTER IN CASTILLE

EYRE
METHUEN

Universitas
BIBLIOTHECA
Ottaviensis

312464

First published 1973
Copyright © 1973 Honor Tracy
Printed in Great Britain
for Eyre Methuen Ltd
11 New Fetter Lane, London EC4P 4EE

SBN 413 29310 6

DP
43
.T 72
1973

Photoset and Printed
by Redwood Press Limited
Trowbridge, Wiltshire

The sun was out all the way from Irun to Madrid: the streams were full and sparkling: the poplars and the birches had their few last leaves atop, like rows of brown brushes dipped in gold paint; and only the lowering blue distances reminded you of winter. But in Madrid itself the rain was pouring vehemently down as if it never meant to leave off.

My former visits to the capital at this time of year had all coincided with spells of good weather, and I had come to think it must be always so. I was looking forward to the lovely pure skies day after day, soft lilac at dawn, then a dazzling blue, orange-pink as evening came. In the sun it would be hot enough to sit out, in the shadow freezing. Hair would crackle under the comb in the crisp dry cold. The people in the streets would move with a springy tread that was far removed from their languid summer dawdle. But now all was grey and weeping, the crowds bedraggled and forlorn, indignant even, like cats who have got a wetting.

It was impossible to find a cab. What with the weather and the new prosperity, the whole enormous fleet appeared to be taken up. Leaving my bags in the cloakroom, I made for the Metro. The cars, dashing through the pools on the road, kept little fountains playing over the pedestrians, who yelled and shook their umbrellas. It was the rush hour and a sodden queue of workers ran all the way up the

Metro stairs and spilled backwards along the pavement. Those who preferred it could get their tickets on a black market informally run by old women: no transaction in Spain is too humble to warrant a fix. The station platform was full to capacity, and so was the train. As it drew up, battle was joined between those wishing to get out and those resolved to get in. In vain did the loudspeaker croak at us to Let Them Off! To and fro the mass of bodies surged, no quarter asked or given. The man in front of me carried a sturdy roll of linoleum, which he used now as a battering-ram, now as a club, to open a passage for us both. Inside the crowd wedged tighter and tighter until I thought my ribs would crack. Involuntary cries of pain or alarm from those new to the Spanish way of life brought sardonic jeers from the rest. One vocal Swede was advised, next time he came to Madrid, to bring his helicopter. A notice forbidding us to buy or sell en route was wholly redundant.

The atmosphere reeked of sweat, tobacco and garlic. Something burrowed frantically against my thigh but, until the train stopped and various people struggled towards the door, I could not even look to see what it was. Then I discovered a tiny boy, making a cage round his head with his arm in order that he might breathe. Either because the carriage was built abroad or from delusions of grandeur, the rail for holding on to was out of reach for Spaniards of average height: one little fellow hung there like a monkey with both feet off the ground. More bodies burst in and the tiny boy began frenziedly burrowing again. But at Puerta del Sol most of the people got out and few came in, so that we now were hardly worse off than in the London rush hour; and the train continued to empty until by the time we reached Ventas, I was actually sitting. Very few seats are installed, and a number of those are reserved for *caballeros mutilados:* for mutilated ladies, there seems to be no provision.

At Ventas I stumbled out with nothing worse than a bruise or two. In accordance with the Keep the City Clean campaign, a new glossy bin was provided for used tickets, and it was charming to see the people hold them ready and then just miss, so that they lay about in drifts on the ground below.

On the recommendation of a friend, I was going to try a residencia in this remote and mainly working-class district on the edge of Madrid, near the bullring, with traces of the Civil War lingering on in broken pavements and damaged houses. As I came out of the Metro station there was a sudden mighty crash. Half the façade of a building had slipped to the ground, narrowly missing a young soldier who, overcome by the experience, had to be helped into a bar and plied with brandy: it was a real *cosa de España*, to welcome a truant back. A similar *cosa* waited at the residencia itself, where the clerk passionately denied having received my request for a booking. Letters do not really go astray in Spain more often than anywhere else, and I pleaded with him to make quite sure, for the prospect of roaming the dismal streets after a long journey in search of a roof was not inviting; but he was deaf to all entreaty.

'Mistakes do not happen here,' he assured me with an offended air.

Perhaps then he would kindly suggest where I could try, since he had nothing for me?

'Who says I have nothing for you?' he demanded. 'There is any amount of room, in fact the place is half empty. But depend upon it, we did *not* receive your letter. Passport, please.'

By the time the forms were filled out, we were the best of friends.

'But you realize, I hope,' he remarked, 'that in no case may you remain here more than a month?'

'Even though you should continue to be half empty?'

'Even then,' he confirmed, with a curious deep satisfaction. And where was my luggage? No, he could not send for it, this was a residencia, not an hotel. For the same reason, no meals were to be had except breakfast, which was served in the bar over there –

and he pointed triumphantly to a door on which hung a placard, Closed Until Further Notice.

Returning from the station with my luggage some time later, I saw that the house with the fallen façade had been roped off. Firemen prowled about the balconies, dislodging more loose plaster with long-handled curly-headed axes, like those of medieval executioners. Passers-by skipped out of harm's way and the landlord, bobbing from side to side in an upper window like Punch in his box, wrung his hands and lamented. All that was wanting now to make me feel entirely at home was a paragraph in the journal which I read at dinner. Headed *Accidents to Lifts*, it ran: 'A house-maid was injured at a house in Islas Filipinas, when the lift fell, the cables having snapped. The frequency of such accidents is causing grave concern.'

After an overland journey from London, I was looking forward to having my sleep out; but at seven o'clock in the morning a prodigious row began in the street below as dust-men emptied the bins. For the first time ever in Spain I heard somebody – a woman, of course, no man would dare – complain of noise. A window flew up and an irate female voice shrieked at them, without the smallest effect beyond adding to the general uproar. Peace came slowly back; but an hour or so later there was another memorable happening. A lorry got stuck across the street, causing a traffic jam some two hundred yards in length; and the driver of every car involved put his thumb on the hooter and kept it there until the lorry managed to move away. In Madrid it is strictly forbidden to sound the hooter at all except in emergency, and I only wished that those who believe Spaniards to be a bullied race, cowering under fascist oppression, could have been there to learn their mistake.

It is strange how memory picks out this and slides over that. The collapse of the house-front, the precipitation of the lift with housemaid, were both so much a part of Spanish life as I knew it; but I had clean forgotten Spanish noise. In the teeth of all experience I had imagined it would be possible to slumber on through the morning until I woke of my own accord. No Spaniard would make such a foolish error, and few are at all aggrieved by the actual event. 'With us, for a guest to wish the cook wouldn't scream seguidillas while he tries to sleep or work is thought excessively, ridiculously soft,' remarks a nineteenth-century writer, quoted by Azorín in his book on Castille; and Azorín has this to say on his own account: 'At any time of the day or night we hear crashes, yells, songs, draggings of furniture. Out in the corridor a steady persistent monotonous chatter prevents our sleeping for hours on end. I have often thought that the degree of sensitivity – and hence of civilization – of any people can partly be measured by the extent to which they will tolerate noise.'

Both gentlemen, of course, wrote in the halcyon days before the telly and the juke-box added their contribution to the prevailing brouhaha. That very morning I was to be in a café which had both going at full tilt together. At one end of the bar was the telly, with a symphony concert in progress: at the other was a film juke-box with half-naked adolescents yelling pop; and in between the barmen were roaring like bulls to make themselves heard. Now and again a snatch of Beethoven was wafted our way, but mostly the conductor appeared to be waving his baton for his own private amusement, while the customers placidly ate and drank and took no notice of either.

Having no appointments before luncheon, I went for a stroll round the quarter. There were signs of improving standards here as well. In the Plaza de Roma the stallholders, the shoe-blacks, even the old women on the kerb with a laundry basket bulging with sweets for sale, had each a howling transistor. Early as it was, the numerous bars were thronged with people enjoying a variety of snacks, boiled mussels stiff with age, tiny roasted larks, cold soggy Spanish omelette, or the viscous porridge called Russian salad; and all, men and women alike, were drinking on a scale that was formerly unheard of.

As always in places of recent affluence, the shops were full of expensive rubbish, weird artefacts such as a stag's

9

antlers polished, mounted and fitted with a clock, an eighteenth-century pistol that, emitting a tongue of flame, would light a cigarette, lampholders in the form of candles with imitation wax running down, doorbells that trilled a merry tune when pressed, and a wicked profusion of wrought iron. There were Christmas cards by the hundred, all with a dire family resemblance, baby-faced Virgins wreathed in vacant smiles, star-spangled heavens, animals out of a Disney cartoon; indeed, the whole collection seemed to bear the Disney imprint. One store had a range of dolls costing up to four hundred pesetas, leering and ogling like Hollywood starlets. Pride of place was given to Bébé, who drank real milk and afterwards did pipi, the last thing one would expect to find in decent Madrid. A little group of old men stood at the window and watched her performance intently.

'It's wonderful, what they think of nowadays,' one remarked.

In search of something less up to the minute, I made my way to the Museo Taurino in the fighters' rooms beside the bullring. Here were reverently displayed the portraits of bulls who had killed some famous *torero* or other, going back over a century and a half, most of them with surprising nicknames, such as Pretty, Pugnose, Box-of-Sweets, although one was called El Miserable: portraits of fighters, including a dwarf, El Enano de la Venta, who in November 1817 bravely sallied into the ring as picador; and the heads of bulls, mounted and presented by some rich noble, gazing down from the wall with an air of invincible stupidity. No such collection, of course, is ever complete without the *traje de luces* worn by a great matador on the day of his death; and here was that of the genius Manolete, lent by General Franco himself.

The highlight of it all was an elaborate model of the ancient ring, with every detail lovingly supplied down to the very gaslights round the exterior walls. It was the work of don Amelio de Arcos Muñoz-Cruzado, gentleman, inspired by his afición to Spain's traditional fiesta, a prodigious pointless labour of love which may well have taken him years.

To express devotion in some absurd exaggerated manner is a characteristic of Spaniards. One thinks of the civil servant Bringas, one of Pérez Galdós's happiest creations, and the work of art he prepared for Mrs Pez (or Fish), in memory of her dead son, woven in four shades of human hair, drawn from the heads of Pez relations. 'It was a – how shall I describe it? – a fine sepulchral design in a highly audacious architectural style, grandiose in plan and rich in ornament. It had pyramidal ramps and Graeco-Roman foundations, and broke out here and there into flying buttresses and parapets, pinnacles, gargoyles and cupolas. Moreover it was completely surrounded by large quantities of torches, urns, vases, owls, wreaths of everlastings, hourglasses, scythes, palm leaves, broken columns and other emblems of Death and Eternal Life.' The cenotaph alone took the whole month of March, and by the middle of April the angel had arms and a head: in June, sad to say, Bringas went blind. But, notes the author, he had 'displayed in it a truly extraordinary ability, a steadiness of hand and sharpness of eye which approached the marvellous – if they did not go a little beyond it.'

Having exhausted the charms of Ventas, I walked through the park of the Buen Retiro to Alfonso XII, the aristocratic thorough-fare which runs along one side of it. On previous visits over the years this had always been up for adjustments to a water main: now the work was done and the road hardly seemed itself without piles of rubble and men in orange jackets warming themselves round a brazier. I was to lunch with a friend whose flat, on the eighth floor, had a delightful roof garden at the back and a view right over the Retiro in front; and it was melancholy to find that beautiful panorama now marred by a hideous box on the other side of the park, towering above the tree tops.

Five years had passed since the two of us had met, but Pilar greeted me as if it were five days. She is a woman of minute physique but remarkably strong character.

11

Estranged from her husband, she had brought up and provided for her five children alone: what with them and the house and her job, an hour's journey away, she used to be up before six and in bed after one. Even in those days the full-time serving women of Madrid, with their long hours and low wages, had all but vanished. Pilar's only help was from a series of *asistentas*, who came in a few hours daily; and a fine assortment they were. There was one whom we called La Goyesca for her resemblance to the guerrilleras in Goya's studies of war: her mouth always hanging open, she sniffed prodigiously, long terrible sniffs, and in a choking voice complained to all around of being *constipada*. That is the Spanish for having a cold in the head, in her case so evident as scarcely to call for mention. Another turned out to be a nun. She had been professed nine years when her mother became an invalid, and the bishop allowed her to re-enter the world for the rest of her mother's life; but she pined for her convent cell.

'I always thought she looked like a nun!' Pilar remarked when the truth came out; and I thought it sharp of her, for the woman looked to me like any other lugubrious 'treasure'.

In spite of that arduous existence, Pilar was always gay, alert and fashionably dressed. The only time her weariness showed was when I took her to a film or a play: then she fell sound asleep. This habit proved a blessing on one occasion, when I invited her to a drama of which excellent reports had been given. It was, in fact, as Spanish films are wont to be, quite awful but interesting in this, that many of the scenes were more appropriate to a Soho club than a family cinema in the heart of Catholic Madrid. One peculiarly vivid sequence was laid in a brothel with burly negroes flogging recalcitrant women, and I shot a nervous glance at Pilar, least narrow-minded of mortals but with a full share of Spanish modesty. She was safe in the land of Nod, however, and afterwards assured me such films were *regular* at the present time: not for the world would she confess that the cream of the spectacle had passed her by.

12

Now the testing days were over. The two boys were doing their military service, one girl was *prometida*, another about to be and the youngest entirely taken up with telephoning and dating. Pilar gave me their news at the kitchen stove while she caressed a huge canary-yellow paella with a wooden fork. Although she has spent her life in Madrid the family is from Seville, and she has all the Sevillan lavishness and enjoyment of good things. Apart from the paella she had provided roast lamb with endive salad, exotic little cakes soaked in rum, enormous Valencia oranges and plenty of good Logroño wine.

'You are much thinner,' Pilar remarked, heaping my plate. 'It suits you, but don't waste away.'

There seemed little prospect of it. During the meal she recounted the doings, often fantastic, of the inhabitants of the house and neighbourhood. A well-known doctor, living a few doors away, had a daughter whom he greatly loved and took everywhere with him. Then she died: whereupon he embalmed her body and continued driving out with it and propping it up beside him at home for months before the death was discovered.

I was able to cap this story from the broad deep well of Spanish oddity with another, that of the fisherman of Almería. He had fallen gravely ill and promised the Virgin that if she helped him recover he would pass the next twenty years at sea in his little boat. He did recover and he fulfilled his vow. For twenty years he was seen bobbing up and down outside the harbour mole: water and provisions were brought to him daily: once a month the barber rowed out to cut his hair and shave his beard; and when he finally stepped ashore to meet the assembled pressmen, he had nothing to say but 'Ah me, the boredom.'

Pilar was delighted with this but pointed out that the vow had been made over twenty years ago. 'It would not happen today,' she declared. 'People no longer take those extravagant pledges. All that is changing with everything else, even among the simplest.' She was probably right: it is rare now to see the purple blouse and yellow cord once commonly

13

worn by men and women accomplishing vovs or in penitence; but it seemed a pity.

Our lunch had begun at the good Spanish hour of three and afterwards we sat on talking until long after darkness fell. Pilar gave me the rest of her family news, no small undertaking as, apart from her children and her mother – a famous character – she had sisters and brothers and so many nephews and nieces I often lost count. Family life in Spain is nothing like ours, with its casual ways, outside interests, free and easy contacts, invitations to people we hardly know. It is a world in itself and more or less a closed one. For a particular reason I had been allowed in this magic circle; but in all the years I have enjoyed the privilege hardly once did I meet anyone there who was not a relation, nor could my friends happily fix their minds for long on any but family matters.

In one respect, however, Pilar is most unSpanish: you can say whatever you like to her. No subject has to be avoided, nor does she ever display that touchy *amour propre* so characteristic of her people. Her own opinions too are given with frankness, and are often unexpected.

'This fuss about Gibraltar,' she remarked at one point. 'Too absurd! We don't really want it at all.'

I was well aware of that. 'Nor do we,' I assured her.

'It's the men, as usual,' she went on. 'Any excuse for kicking up a row!'

We cursed the sex for a while with keen enjoyment.

When at last I took my leave the weather had changed and it was a lovely frosty moonlit night for walking home. There was a magic beauty about the Retiro, lights sparkling through the trees in the little avenue leading to the plaza Nicaragua with its ghostly white fountain: that and the pale urns and the stone figures of kings and princes gave it the air of a brilliant setting for some play just about to begin. The pose of the statues, including that of the Batallador and other warlike persons, was curiously languid compared with the martial stance of Alfonso XII, known as the Peacemaker, high on his horse over the lake. Despite the

14

hour the gate was open and I turned in, meaning to wander about and look at the moon in the water; but I was hailed at once by a passer-by of that benevolent species which takes every foreigner under its wing.

'On no account go in there,' he commanded. 'You would meet with bad characters.'

The park seemed to be wholly deserted and I have never met any bad characters in Madrid. I told him as much, and it pleased him, but he was adamant I should not go in. You have to accustom yourself, in Spain, to people making decisions for you: accordingly, I renounced the little pleasure and he went his way, gleeful as the victor in a game of chess.

The next day was El Día del Emigrante, when all over the land prayers are offered and collections made for Spaniards working abroad. In my experience, these have always set off with alacrity and written home cheerful accounts of foreign life and wages; but the official line is that they are reluctant exiles, wandering in tears amid the alien corn.

A beautiful day, warm and sunny as April in the south, had brought the collectors out in droves, foiling with practised skill every attempt to dodge them. Smart young women from Acción Católica were the most proficient. Their technique, simple but effective, was to sail in and plant the flag, neatly as a *banderilla*, in the lapel of someone's coat. The victim, always male, was never so ungallant as to return it and, good humoured, resigned or fretful, would dig in his pocket for change. Although a generous people, Spaniards do not take kindly to collections: you may sit at the back of any crowded church and by the time the offertory basket arrives the contents would hardly buy you a breakfast.

I was on my way to the Rastro, passing through the Plaza Mayor, which looked its best with one end of the rosy façade in brilliant sun, the other in deep shadow. In former days this large and finely proportioned place was used for all manner of public spectacles, from royal bullfights to autos da fé. These last did not involve the burning of heretics, as many people suppose, but were an open recantation of heresy by the penitent, and not half such a draw. Now it was the scene of a bustling market, with booth after booth selling coins or foreign stamps, especially the latter, which seem to be a national craze. I have been asked for them by waiters, hairdressers, taxi-drivers and even policemen. Hundreds of people, young and old, mostly men, crowded round, searching, comparing, bargaining, with the gravity of demeanour they maintain in all transactions, however frivolous.

There was an even greater scrimmage in the Rastro, a kind of Flea Market offering a notable range of services. Spectacles are supplied or adjusted here without tedious medical formalities: keys of every shape and size are cut while you wait; and you may buy clothing, jewellery, toys, furniture, live river crabs, antiques, boots or works of art. A small boy cleared a path through the mob by means of piercing howls as he struggled along with an iron bedstead balanced on his head: an American bought a worthless imitation of a Talavera jug for eight hundred and fifty pesetas. Up a lane at the further end was a bird market, with tiny gaily-coloured birds fluttering despondently in cages fastened to the wall in full sun. One of these was packed so tight that the little creatures could neither stand up nor turn round, and it was pitiful to see the little beaks shoot in and out of the bars as if imploring help. There were also a few puppies for sale, caressed by the passers-by just as they would be in England; but they were apathetic under it all, evidently having no great confidence in the future.

This market must be worth someone's while or it would not be held; but I saw only one purchase made, of a small parroquet by a student, who was wonderfully solemn about it. Most people seemed to be there for the two great pastimes of watching and talking. And a marvellous collection they were, these working-class men and women of Madrid, with their strong severe features: many of them looked positively wild, prepared at any moment to sally forth with pike and axe for another Second of May. One felt, as seldom one feels in London now, that here was race: here were the people whom Goya painted and Borrow extolled, changed but little if at all. In such an assembly I was a conspicuous figure, regarded by the vendors as lawful prey. A foreigner might not suppose she shared the privilege of looking on without buying, and the onslaughts became so vehement that very soon I took to my heels.

There was still time in the long Spanish morning to visit the Convent of the Descalzas Reales, which stands between Arenal and the Gran Via in a small distinguished square, a haven of calm and peace amid the hubbub of the city. I approached it by way of the Calle San Martin, a quiet eighteenth-century street running up from the turbulent Arenal. Above the name on the wall there are tiles depicting Saint Martin on horseback, dividing his cloak with the beggar. Such tiles are an attractive feature of old Madrid – the Calle de los Bordaderos, for example, shows two people hard at work embroidering – and no doubt were of practical use in that illiterate age as well.

Turning into the square, I accidentally knocked into a rosy little old gentleman and excused myself, which led to conversation. He wanted first to know what I thought of Spain and next where I was from: animated by the replies, he forcefully declared that Spain and England must be friends, the Rock must not come between them, their flags must fly there proudly side by side and Gibraltar become the centre of the world.

'I am no longer able to visit London, as I used,' he went on. 'If I were, I would call on your Queen and make my sentiments known.'

Now he fumbled in a pocket and brought out a visiting card, with the name Pedro Guillen Figueros and an address in San Bernardo. 'Do come and see me' he said, 'we can discuss these things at our leisure.' He fumbled in another pocket and fished up a scribbled note. 'This was in a letter, but I cannot read English,' he continued, holding it to his eyes and then out to me. 'Qué suerte, my running across you. Please translate.'

The Governor appreciates your kindly thought in writing to him but at present can think of no position suited to your talents or that would interest you. He wishes you all success in the search for what you want.

If don Pedro was disappointed, he bore it well.

'So that is that,' he remarked.

Which Governor was this?

'Rockefeller, Governor of New York,' he replied, with a certain grandiloquence. But he must not delay me further. Was I going to the convent? There were many fine things to see in Madrid, but none to compare with those of his native Granada. And with a further invitation to visit his house, he toddled away.

The convent is a handsome dignified building of the sixteenth century, founded by doña Juana, daughter of Carlos V and sister of Philip II, as a refuge from the stresses and strains of the Court. A pibture of her by Sanchez Coello presents a saturnine young woman with a long sharp nose and the air of one who will stand no nonsense: the little terrier in her lap looks infinitely more agreeable. Born in 1535, at seventeen she married the Crown Prince of Portugal, don Juan Manuel, was left a widow after eleven months and had a son, Sebastian, who later became the Portuguese king and hero of fantastic legends. She had outstanding gifts, intellectual and artistic, and ably governed the state for several years while her father and brother were abroad. After her death at the Escorial in 1573, her body was removed to this convent and buried in a tomb built to her specification: Spaniards of high degree who scorn the world are curiously particular about the housing of their remains once they leave it for good.

Her confessor was Francisco de Borja, who began life as a duke and finished up as a saint. On his advice doña Juana chose the order of Franciscanas Clarisas, or Poor Clares, vowed to poverty, humility, perpetual fasting and abstinence, bare feet and strict enclosure. But in the first two centuries of the convent's life so many women of royal or aristocratic birth were professed that it rapidly filled up with splendid treasures and works of art. Today it is a

19

museum, part of the Patrimonio Nacional, benevolently supervised by father-figures of the State: there still are thirty nuns, no longer aristocratic but rigidly enclosed as ever, so that certain treasures only may be viewed and these not every day.

There was no one else in the ante-room, and the guide said we must wait until others arrived: much of life in Spain consists of waiting. 'And smoking is not allowed,' he added, although I had given no sign of it: 'Remember please that here is *clausura*.' Through the open door I could hear another guide chatting away to the nuns, so that the *clausura* was evidently not as strict as all that: indeed, the male attendants about the place seemed to enjoy the cosy position of eunuchs in a harem. At intervals people trickled in by twos and threes, till finally there were enough to form a *grupo* and we set off on our tour.

The time allowed for visiting this very rich, in fact sumptuous, palace was twenty-five minutes. The guide whisking us round was a plump fellow in fine livery, with the deportment of a Hollywood butler. He associated himself with the place completely: if we exclaimed in wonder or admiration his bosom swelled and his eye flashed as if he had been the artist. Nor did he appear to think of us as travellers anxious to see what was beautiful or of interest wherever we went but rather, as converging from the four quarters of the globe on this particular spot, after saving up to do so all our lives.

He proved a severe master: we had to trot, docile, at his heels, stragglers being frowned on and urged forward by an imperious wave of the hand. As we went, he boomed out a set piece: to questions, he made no reply. There was no hope of consulting the book I had with me, for the flock would be out of sight before I could turn up the page. It was like watching a film that ran at twice the normal speed. A Rubens flashed past, a gold chalice studded with emeralds shot up, royal portraits dizzily followed each other, Christ agonized for a moment, on one of the Eucharistic tapestries two voluptuous girls, attended by cherubs, played half a bar on cello and lute, Zurbarán's St Francis prayed and

Pedro de Mena's *Dolorosa* grieved while we sped by regardless.

Once the guide called a sudden halt by a window overlooking the convent garden and pointed dramatically through it. 'The Galerias Preciados!' he said in triumph; and so indeed it was, Madrid's mammoth store, hideously rising above the mellow roofs and spires and turrets. But there was no lingering even here; on we swept and in next to no time found ourselves again in the ante-room, where our mentor, now wreathed in smiles, awaited his due reward.

One clear memory stays with me, of the many enchanting statues and portraits of children with which these childless women had surrounded themselves. Over and over again appeared the Child with Skull, symbol of life and death, the skull used now as a plaything, now as a pillow. There were two little daughters of Philip II, painted by Sanchez Coello in the stiff bejewelled brocades that Infantas wore from the time they began to toddle, their round faces sweetly blank; and two small sons of the same, beruffed and beskirted, grasping rods of office with an air of precocious authority. Most appealing of all was a carving of the boy Jesus in Meditation, attributed to Alonso Cano, seated with closed eyes in a chair, one chubby hand supporting a chubby cheek, the other resting on the globe, and looking like nothing so much as a naughty Spanish choirboy snoozing through a sermon.

Otherwise I took nothing away but an assortment of vivid but fleeting impressions. It was disappointing, but the nuns no doubt would feel we were lucky to get in at all. Living in their splendid past, they would regard all this wealth as the patrimony of the Order, not of the nation. Our intrusion was the price they paid for survival, and nuns have a way of beating prices down.

In a street to one side of the convent was a tavern of enticing appearance, the Meson de las Descalzas, with plaited wreaths of garlic, jars of wine and mounds of pink juicy shellfish in the window. I went in for a glass of rosado and a tapa of prawns, and was nicely gypped, being charged the equivalent of eighty-five new pence. That kind of thing was formerly rare in Madrid, as in most parts of the country: the two exceptions were Cataluña, where they cheat for love of money, and Galicia, where they cheat for love of cheating. Other Spaniards despised it, and the less they had the more utterly honest they were: it is only now, with prosperity, that gypping has come into fashion.

The waiter was fashionable too, with long hair and pointed shoes, but his reply to my complaint was in the old tradition.

'Prawns are dear,' he said. 'They are seventy pesetas a hundred grammes. And you had two.'

'Excuse me, there were only nine or ten of them.'

'Exactly. Two hundred grammes.'

'I am accustomed to marketing. I know what prawns weigh. There would be twelve or so in a hundred grammes.'

'Yours were particularly large. They weighed two hundred grammes.'

There was nothing to be done. You can scare a Catalan with threats of Turismo or simply argue a Gallego down, but once the Madrileño has taken a stand, however absurd, he never retreats.

There were no disagreeable surprises at the Callejon, where I went for lunch. Tucked away in a narrow turning off Preciados, out of the tourist stream, unadvertised, it is one place in Madrid that never changes. The doorman remarked he had not seen me for some little time, in other words, five years. All the old waiters were there, the simple decent furniture had not been smartened up, the walls still were hung with signed photographs of dancers, *toreros* and other notables, there was the same friendly welcome. And the same lavishness: as I sat down an old gentleman was fretting over a custard pear, saying it was very small, whereupon an entire bowl of custard pears was hurriedly placed before him. No one here, for sure, has ever so much as seen a paper napkin.

22

'So you're back again,' said my waiter, bustling up. 'It's red wine for you, verdad?'

How Spanish waiters can remember all they do is a puzzle, but it makes for happy contented clients.

Afterwards I went to a film which had been causing no little stir. It was partly the work of the well-known producer and cartoonist Manuel Summers, who loves sailing close to the wind: indeed, before the winter was out, a page of satirical drawings about the First Assembly of Bishops and Priests in Madrid had earned him three months and a day in gaol and six years and a day *inhabilitación*, a bar from participation in any cultural work subsidized by the State; which, as films are mostly State-subsidized now, must have left him on pretty short commons.

All that still lay in the future, however, and at the present time he was enjoying an immense *succès de scandale*.

After the news, consisting as usual of the triumphs scored by the regime, and a protracted interval, while the audience ran about in search of toffee or Coca Cola, we finally got down to *Adiós, Ciqüeños, Adiós!* The theme, as the title suggests, was the death of childish innocence; and firstly came a quotation from St Augustine, implying that anyone who found impurity in what would follow must be himself impure.

A fifteen-year-old boy is madly in love with a girl of thirteen. On a school expedition to the mountains they get separated from the others and spend some time in a hut; and although the girl knows nothing and the boy little more, the result is a baby. To conceal this from her family, she pretends to be invited for a long stay in the country: in fact she moves to a derelict attic, which a gang of smaller children furnish by stealing, and settles down to wait, mystified by her growing tummy and with no idea of what lies ahead. Here, surrounded by the gang, shouting, weeping and offering advice, she eventually brings forth, in a scene which spares the onlooker nothing. A tense few moments occur when the baby fails to move or cry, but at last it begins to bawl and, to the strains of the Hallelujah chorus, the film fades out.

It was mild enough by contemporary standards, but a mawkish affair, the adults, whether parents, teachers or clergy, being stupid, querulous, unconcerned or defeated, the young lovers all sweet innocence, the other children more generous and loving than seemed quite possible. As with so much Spanish work today, in films, novels or plays, there was a total absence of mind. No problems were faced, nor doubts answered: the message appeared to be, that a birth was absolutely good in itself, whatever the circumstances. Yet it was startling to find it shown here, where until recently the most harmless films were given ecclesiastical grading, *autorizada, tolerada, prohibida* and so on; and even more, that the cinema was full of the middle-class middle-aged who would formerly cluck and hiss at the faintest impropriety. Truly, had it not been for the peals of laughter at the more agonized moments of parturition, I would hardly have known the audience was Spanish at all.

It was still chuckling reminiscently as we made our way out, the Hallelujah chorus booming after us. A long impatient queue had assembled for the next performance. As it was Sunday evening, all Madrid was going somewhere, dressed up to the nines. Taxis went by in an endless stream, loaded with family parties. Cars shot round the fountain of Cibeles and up the Alcalá, like beetles frantic with marijuana. The jets were playing and the water was lit up, in fact all that could be illuminated was, including those groups of romantic or classical statuary that perch on the roofs of banks and business houses, incongruous as the birds or flowers on a dowager's hat.

Strolling along the Gran Via, I caught sight of a motorist turning her car into a one-way street, to face a long line of approaching traffic, and I stopped in pleasant anticipation. There is always more fun in the streets of Madrid than in her centres of formal entertainment. The rightful users of the way all burst out hooting together, to which she responded grimly and steadily, as if hoping in time to bring them round. An impasse seemed to be reached; but then, all at once, with a disdainful shrug, she accepted defeat and backed with tremendous verve into the Gran Via again, just as the lights turned green and a solid phalanx of vehicles thundered up the hill towards her. It was like a child on a pony, backing across a cavalry charge. The air was rent with the squeals of brakes and roars of fury. Calm and unhurrying, she swung the car round, changed gear, executed a series of froggish leaps, and stalled. Pandemonium broke out once more.

I had been looking on up to this with detached amusement, a mere spectator, but now as she sat there, tentatively pulling this and prodding that, I remembered having met her once or twice, some years ago, at the house of a friend. There was no mistaking the hawkish profile, the mane of springy white hair and the absolute self-assurance. I remembered too a discussion, or rather an address given by her, on the subject of contemporary women, their drinking, their smoking, and their habit of flying about, as God had never intended they should, in automobiles. Motoring, she had laid it down, was exclusively for men, and she would rather see any daughter of hers perform in a circus.

When finally the engine started and she had leisure to look about her again, she saw me standing there and with a friendly smile of recognition pulled into the kerb across the bonnet of a taxi and halted under a no-parking sign.

'Long time no see,' she called out, in her husky baritone: she had a fund of colloquial English phrases, *use your loaf, blow me down, pardon my glove*, and so forth. 'And how do you find Madrid?' she continued, in Spanish.

'There seem rather a lot of changes.'

'Ya lo creo! It becomes impossible to get about. Did you see me turn into the Calle de Silva? I always go up it, as a short cut home. They have changed it since this morning. Now I must go all the way to the . . . '

'Doña Prudencia, excuse me, I think there's a guardia coming . . . '

'Oh? then I'll hop it,' she said, lapsing into her second

tongue. 'Be seeing you one of these days. Chin chin!'

And away she went, followed by passionate blasts on the *guardia's* whistle.

Yes, changes were in the air. Literally so, for early one morning, before the fumes of petrol and diesel oil took over, I caught a whiff of that fragrance, compounded of mist and grime, which formerly was so marked a feature of wintry London. Here of all places was good authentic smog, stinging the eyes and burning the throat, witness to the triumph of industrialization; and the sharp tang of it called up remembrances of things past as vivid in their way as those of Proust, munching his famous little cake.

And then I read that all the cows are to be removed from the city. This was decided long ago, but there were so many of them that ten years' grace was allowed for the making of other arrangements. In future milk, weeks old and laced with preservative, will doubtless arrive from far away in huge containers, according to modern practice. The last little countrified touch will disappear from Madrid, where rustic scenes were once so plentiful and so charming. Every Wednesday morning herds of goats and flocks of sheep used to patter down the Alcalá, and traffic was constantly slowed up by wooden carts, piled with fodder, rumbling placidly along the elegant boulevards in their own good time; and country people came riding by on mules, as much at their ease as in the lanes of their own pueblo.

Landmarks vanish all the time, replaced by trendy affairs that swiftly vanish too. On a previous visit I lamented finding my favourite bootblack parlour superseded by a

27

milkbar, all hygienic and horrid. Now this had gone and in its place was a boutique catering for sophisticated dogs. As well as fancy leads, collars and woolly garments, it provided all manner of 'amusing' rubber toys, a sausage, a shoe, a rabbit, a slice of chocolate cake and – for we may trust the Spanish to introduce a macabre note – the severed head of a cat. Not far from this again was the store where I used to feast my eyes on a wondrous array of traditional headgear, from the Cardinal's scarlet hat to the bullfighter's trim little bonnet. Now it was mainly given over to glossy velour creations of bourgeois design, but in the middle, as exhibit number one, was a shapeless fur cap with the recommendation: Imported from the People's Republic of China. And with that, I felt I had seen about everything.

More important, and very fascinating, is the remarkable change in physique. The rising generation, those in their middle and late teens, are so much taller than their parents that they almost seem of a different nationality. Better food and more athletics are creating a new race. It was nicely illustrated one day, on a platform in the Metro, when a group of tubby little middle-aged men, of the strutting moustache-twirling kind, were throwing glances at some schoolgirls, every one a good head taller than the would-be don Juans and taking not the least notice of them. And the girls' indifference was symptomatic too, for there was nothing assumed or coquettish about it, as in days gone by. They were intent on their own concerns, without a thought to spare for their midget admirers, who sighed, coughed and whistled in vain.

Male privilege is dwindling fast, and male strongholds, once all but impregnable, are not only invaded but taken over. There is a café off the Gran Via where I had long been used to meeting friends or colleagues, and usually was the only woman present. It had a stand-up bar and behind this an inner sanctum with chairs and tables, always full of men talking business or reading newspapers. They would look up as I came in, plainly disapproving but politely removing their hats nevertheless. Dropping in to see if anyone known to me was there, I found it wholly occupied by girls, some in trousers, some in mini-skirts, playing poker, throwing dice or merely shouting, many of them half-seas-over. The aged waiter, a relic of other times, stood looking on with folded arms, his face grim, his lips moving in secret denunciation.

It would have been interesting to know how these girls had so much leisure and so much money, but I lacked the gall to inquire. The confidence of Mass Observers and Social Surveyors, their fearless interrogation of total strangers, alas, are beyond me. Yet much, even perhaps as much, may be learned by simply using the eyes. At any hour of the day the bars of Madrid were brimming with young, in high spirits and spending freely, whether in the smart haunts on the boulevards or those of humble degree, with their deafening jukes and the eternal ping-ping-ping of fruit machines. It seemed a revolution almost in itself.

A visit to the University, however, made a very different impression. The site is beautiful, at the point beyond Argüelles where the city ends abruptly, without suburban tailing-off or ribbon development. Wide rolling country starts at once – although dotted now with many a giant eyesore – against the splendid background of the Sierras. In the University itself there is a great feeling of space, with ample lawns and well-kept gardens planted with trees and flowering shrubs. The schools are deplorable, stark hideous boxes that would do as well for factories or prisons, as if the architects had failed to grasp the difference.

It was, however, the students that I had come to see, and, accustomed to the home-bred species, I would hardly have guessed they were students at all. To a man, they were clean, tidy and well turned out. There were no carnival get-ups or yobo jeans, no matted locks à la Rasputin, no beards like a derelict busby. But there was no gaiety either, no joking or horseplay, no youthful ebullience. Boys and girls alike, they looked gloomy, downcast, even sullen, hardly exchanging a word as they trooped along to their classes. The contrast between them and the convivial sprites of Madrid was fantastic. Perhaps, to adapt the lines of Blake, it was a simple case of

> Dear mother, dear mother, the classroom is cold
> But the alehouse is healthy and pleasant and warm . . .

Perhaps some untoward event had cast a shadow on that particular day, perhaps a crucial examination loomed ahead. One should not leap to hasty conclusions, but I did spend a whole morning there without seeing one really cheerful face.

On wall after wall the students had painted slogans in red, and these had been heavily painted over in black, so as to be almost illegible. Here and there one could make out a word or two, *Revolution*, or *Down with*. . . . On one of the stone benches in a little formal garden between Farmacia and Medicina was a message in red chalk that the authorities had left untouched: 'Carlismo, sí! Marxismo, no!' and on another, which they had possibly overlooked: 'Franco asesino!'

Except for this last, which after all was true, I saw nothing but what might be scribbled up in Oxford, Cambridge, London or any English seat of learning. Students dream of society turned upside down and heads a-roll, just as imaginative children orphan themselves, to gain a wider scope for their fantasies. What exactly they have in mind, what form their revolution should take, above all how they are to achieve it, they would be puzzled to say and probably do not much care. It all belongs to happy carefree subsidized youth. But the Spanish authorities are as down on them as any inquisitor sniffing out heresy. Today, in the very centre of the campus, stood two lorries, each with a crew of *policias armadas*, those in the grey uniform who are concerned with political matters. A little further on, by the Faculty of Science, was another car with more of the same. One of them, in riot gear, was posted at the door, checking all who went in or out. Presently a dozen or more, also in shock helmets, surged into the building together, batons in hand. Meanwhile students paced up and down outside, talking in low voices, as if this performance were nothing out of the way.

All in all, it was a depressing experience. I did find one morsel of comic relief, but it had nothing to do with the students or the faculty or the police or Madrid or, indeed, with anything whatsoever. This was a monument, gift of the American lady who had conceived and executed it. A naked man on horseback was bending down to receive a flaming torch from a stricken hero, who lay writhing on the ground in agony; and on the plinth, in English, a poem was engraved:

> Man bears the holy torch fidelity
> Across the burning sands of time,
> A woman's soul uplifts maternity,
> A torch to light a path no less sublime!
> A desperate endeavour of the soul!
> It is a holy path these two have trod
> To light the way to one eternal goal
> And stand before the gorgeous door of God.

The first and last names of the poet were indecipherable, but the middle one, appropriately enough, was Milton.

What was up in the Unversity that day I never found out. Friends shrugged it off as *regular* and the newspapers kept mum. They usually do unless the gravity of affairs – or, plainly put, the number of witnesses – forces their hand, and even then they are careful to avoid sensationalism. A curt paragraph announces that a number of protesting students, or workers, were quickly and quietly dispersed by the *fuerzas publicas*: the charges, the clubbings, the broken heads, the occasional death, are passed over, no doubt as 'colour stuff' unworthy of a sober factual press.

In this department at least there has been no change at all. Except for growing steadily duller, the newspapers remain as they were, high, mighty and chronically misinformed as to foreign affairs, euphoric as to their own. Panegyrics on Church and State are automatic, and you automatically skip them, but they are bestowed as well, left and right, on books, plays, music and bullfights that are equally undeserving. And the singular part of it is, that when you meet a journalist his talk, like that of most Spaniards, is ironic, astringent and even biting; but let him put pen to paper and off he goes, in the fulsome flowery style of an apprentice hagiographer.

This is not to say that the darker side is wholly ignored. Crimes will be shortly noted, but it is curious how often they seem to occur in another part of the country. The Madrid papers will carry news of goings-on in Barcelona, and the other way round. An exception is Málaga, where ample coverage is given to local delinquents, these however being invariably foreign and in a state of *embriaguez*. Accordingly, it came as a surprise when I was attacked there once by two youths, neither foreign nor drunk, and robbed of my purse. It was a further surprise when the local police reacted to the information as to a familiar routine, and a greater one still when all our Consul had to say was 'Oh.. Not another!' As far as I remember, it was his third case that month, one of the victims being still in hospital; but there had not been a line about them in the press.

And the papers kick up all kinds of little fusses, to assure the public they are on their toes. Since every subject of real importance is tabu, these are trifling or peripheral, a pounce on little men who cannot hit back or on something so vague and general there is no hitting back at all. Fearless indictments are made of bunglings or inconveniences that are so much a part of Spanish life as to be barely worth recording. On a front page one day there was splashed the word INCREDIBLE! It related to a level-crossing on the Zaragoza-Miranda line which had been shut for two whole hours, while the queue of waiting motorcars grew longer and longer. The railwaymen could do nothing, having no telephone and hence no means of communicating with other stations; and, as there was a dense fog the gates had to remain closed until the Zaragoza express, invariably late, had gone by. And this on the highway from Madrid to France! and in the holiday season! Foreigners involved!

Furious exchanges between the motorists and the officials! There was nothing incredible about it whatsoever: I have waited six hours in a train ere this, waiting for something or other to happen.

Now and again a paper like the *ABC* really pitches in. It had dutifully reported, in extenso, a speech by the Vice President of the Government to the National Council of the Falange Movement, wherein, amid fervent applause, all the old clichés were trotted out on the old familiar theme: La Salud Politica de la Nacion es Buena. Two days later, however, it carried an article pointing out that the number of prostitutes, aged from fifteen to fifty, had increased by six per cent in the year: that there were now two million alcoholics: that homosexuality was rife: that abortions were common: that pornography was an organized industry; and that the use of drugs had gone up by one hundred per cent. But that was once in a way, and such comment as I heard was mainly disapproving. Spaniards lose no sleep over the state of the nation, its morals, drugs, pornography, drink, or anything else but what directly touches themselves and their families; and they have no affection for simple candour. They prefer the Government fairy tales, not out of wishful thinking, but as something written in a code which they can enjoyably crack. One of the satirical papers had a cartoon which expresses their feeling perfectly: it was of a man opening a newspaper and calling to his wife, 'Bring me my other spectacles, Maria, the ones for reading between the lines.'

There was no call for these useful aids, however, when it came to foreign affairs. Here the press could write freely, since no one cared a button. On the subject of Ireland, for instance, it was enough to make a cat not merely laugh but roll about on the floor. To a man, it applauded that very same marxist/anarchist republican terror from which Spain herself – as it always averred – had only been saved by the combined forces of Franco and God, and those very same aspirations which at home were regarded as treason and dealt with firmly. Thus, on a single page, one could read an admiring report of new savageries by the IRA, always described as the *patriotas*, and a denunciation of two young Basques who had placed a little bomb in a Falange centre, injuring no one and causing about £300 worth of damage, and who, incidentally, were both condemned by a military court to twenty years in gaol. No one saw the absurdity of it, and reasoning was a waste of time: the press believed the IRA was defending the Faith, and once the Faith has been cited, Spaniards stop thinking altogether.

As for the correspondents' despatches, they were a feast in themselves. Even the serious *ABC* took its news from their man in London, who, prudent or economical, followed the entire campaign from that rather distant viewpoint; and the rest relied on informants whose knowledge of either country appeared of the scantiest. The Bogside would turn up in Belfast, while the Falls Road was translated to Derry: The RUC would figure as 'the dread soldiers of Ulster': a piece in *Time* magazine was ascribed to 'that experienced American commentator, Mr. Honor Balfour': Mr David Frost, having apparently quoted a foreign view of the British as cold and hypocritical, was promoted to 'one of the profoundest, most perceptive, observers of the day': the photograph of a trim little suburban street, trees and all, had the caption 'typical Catholic ghetto of Belfast', and so on and so on.

But, turning to lighter things, let there be praise where praise is due. I have said that Spanish papers are dull and rigidly controlled, and so they are. Nevertheless, in a Sunday supplement of the *ABC*, I once came on a piece which was not only hilarious but which no free English paper would be likely to print. This was the report of a round-table conference on the fashions of the day, those taking part being mostly young designers, models and actresses, with one senior person, a well known sculptor. This gentleman had somehow got the idea that they had met to discuss the bullfight and, as he was extremely deaf, it was anything but easy to put him right. With everyone poised to begin, he held things up by asking fretfully over and over again why the bullfight critic, Diaz-Cañabate, had not put in an appearance.

'And Caña? Where is Caña?'

One of the actresses, punning on Caña and *cana* (a 'bock'), requested·a servant to bring the señor some beer.

'What!' cried the sculptor. 'What is Caña up to, drinking beer at this time of day? Really, there's no making the fellow out. Giving himself up to beer at such a moment, late for the conference . . . '

Someone else remarked, she did not see where Caña came in.

'Qué dice? Qué dice?'

The remark was repeated, with greater distinctness.

'This señorita is very pretty, but also a little odd, since naturally when we speak of bulls Caña must have his say.' The sculptor then launched into a diatribe on the iniquity of shaving horns and the disgracefully small and immature bulls that appeared in the ring today.

'This very charming señor talks of nothing but bulls,' a member of the panel observed, 'although we are here to discuss the present fashions, and in particular, hot pants.'

'Qué dice! Qué dice? Hot pants!' the sculptor exploded. 'The last straw! About all that was lacking in the modern torero! To enter the arena in hot pants would turn the national fiesta into a mockery. The things people think of now . . . '

The panel now set to work in earnest to clarify matters, and the sculptor finally grasped what they were supposed to be discussing.

'That is different, excuse me,' he said. 'Cañabate is always disparaging me, pretending that I am deaf, but it is true, I am a little hard of hearing in one ear.' He then gave it as his opinion that women had never been as attractively dressed as today, since the more they revealed of their charms the better he liked it. But while he realized now that clothes were the main topic, he still assumed that these were only such as ladies wore to bullfights. Really, he found it rather absurd. On the whole, he would have done better to stay at home and get on with his sculptings of gypsies.

'But,' said the actress, slowly and clearly, 'bullfights don't enter into it at all. We are to consider the new fashion, and especially hot pants.'

'En minipantalon? No, señorita. I sculpt them naked, or in their traditional costume, in hot pants never. But why, why, does everyone here keep on and on about these hot pants?'

With that, he repeated his views on the modern bull, its horns, size, weight and age; and the conference came to an end.

The audacity of the editor fairly took my English breath away. Censorship, after all, is not solely carried out by official satraps. Such things as the law of libel, the risk of public displeasure, not to speak of taste, delicacy, consideration for the feelings of others, can be every bit as cramping; and, happily impervious to them all, the *ABC* went marching on.

With regard to the bullfighting world, here too a change was looming up that threatened its very foundation. I do not refer to the decadence of the art itself, lamented by the sculptor, but to the liability of *toreros* to income tax. This is something frowned on by Spaniards of every description, as being in fundamental conflict with their way of life. In despair of ever getting true returns of income, the authorities had seized on 'visible signs of wealth' as one basis for assessment; but for the Spaniard there is no point in wealth if it is not to be visible, exposed, flaunted and envied. And this is particularly true of the *torero*: swagger goes with the job. He has to be special, apart, unlike the rest or, rather, the epitome of them. The people do not resent this, they like it. But now, instead of boasting his millions, he has to make out he hardly knows which way to turn for bread. Officialdom sets up its own dreary kind of Frogs' Chorus, the *torero* must pay like anyone else, like anyone else, like anyone else – but he is not like anyone else, nor ever can be as long as Spain is Spain. And if, as now appears to be her ambition, she becomes just another modern society, one more producing-consuming ant-hill, he must quit the scene altogether. He personifies immemorial Spanish things, supremacy of the individual, absolute worth of the human being, stoic courage, the tragic sense of life: in a cosy world with all the paths mapped out and solutions provided on request, that function will disappear.

To have the Escorial to yourself, except for the men in blue and gold, choose a Monday morning in November. I set off early by the tranvia, the clean quick electric train which has superseded the old puff-puff with its acrid smoke and long unscheduled pauses. The only drawback was the freezing cold, for the tranvia apparently warms up as it goes along and by the time the temperature was bearable we had reached our destination. A burly priest in a beret ran up and down, roaring 'There must be a window open! Close it, someone, do! I am cold, cold!' as if the weather had singled him out for special treatment, or he were the only one whose comfort mattered. There was plenty to watch, the coaches being long and open and interconnected. Now and again children were sick, so soon after the train started that they must have decided on it before. A jolly fat man came down the aisle, laughing and joking, and distributed caramels to all who would take them. Having thus created a certain amount of goodwill, he put the sweets away and opened a basket of toys and flowers, all in plastic and stridently coloured, which he offered for sale. At this, sucking their free toffees, everyone looked out of the window and the jollity died away. Next a one-legged man in ragged clothes came in and started giving out holy pictures, which is the tolerated form of begging. Now all the ladies in black reached for their purses, while the salesman bitterly watched the peg-leg reaping where he had sown.

They finished up in a corner, quarrelling all the way to their journey's end.

Presently we slid round the last curl in the track and San Lorenzo de el Escorial came into view. There are few things more dramatic than the sudden appearance of this great monastery, dominating from its perch on the hill the little town below, with the gaunt slopes of the Guadarrama rising behind. Winter was a good time to see it, with the leaves off the trees and the grim bare spaces lying exposed. It had come on to rain, but I went up on foot, the best way of approach but one I could never attempt in the heats of summer.

For all it was a November Monday morning, there were numbers of guides about the courtyard, who at once darted towards me like a shoal of minnows. One of them easily outstripped the others and was taken on. He described himself as a student, but I could not help thinking his studies had been strangely protracted as, apart from his wedding ring and receding hair, he told me he had once guided Hemingway. He annoyed me somewhat by his insistence that, as an Englishwoman, I should have an English-speaking guide: it must have been clear that I was at home in Castilian, and his English was even harder to follow than most. But this apparent pigheadedness had a perfectly simple reason behind it: who understood whom did not signify, but as an English-speaking guide he could charge me more.

'So now you understand,' he said, satisfied of the argument's being conclusive.

But how would it be if he got the English rate and yet spoke Castilian?

He sniffed round the proposition a while, as a dog sniffs an unfamiliar food, and then cautiously said it might do.

The monastery and all to do with it is wonderfully characteristic of this nation. To begin with, it was built to redeem a vow. While the Spanish army (or rather, the army of Spain, for it was composed of and led by foreigners) prepared to attack the French at St Quentin in 1557, the pious but timid Philip II was praying, doing penance and swearing never to fight again should victory be his. He turned to St Lawrence for special assistance, the battle being fought on his day, with the inducement of a monastery if this were effective. St Lawrence was one of the countless Iberian martyrs of the Roman occupation, grilled on a slow fire in 261. Grilling and baking – and even devilling, for mustard and vinegar were applied now and then – were a favourite Roman means of dispatching Christians, who frequently showed an amazing fortitude: St Lawrence, in particular, laughed and joked throughout, inviting his cooks to turn him when one side was sufficiently done and urging them to have a taste. Now, thirteen centuries later, he rallied to the Spanish cause: the day was won and Philip kept his word, as to the foundation, that is. He may have crossed his fingers while vowing to fight no more.

The site he chose could not have been more out of the way or inconvenient: he is said to have picked it because the mountains would furnish stone for the building, although practical considerations were the last to strike him as a rule. The work was begun by Juan Bautista de Toledo in 1563 and finished by Juan de Herrara in 1584, with a labour force of three thousand to be housed and fed in this desert miles from anywhere. The architects were men of genius and money flowed like water; but the king directed and supervised, and the result was a vast gloomy grey barracks of lead, slate and granite with row upon row of tiny blank windows, suggestive of a prison. Apart from its huge bulk, the most remarkable thing about it is a curious timeless quality: Ford, writing in 1845, commented on its looking new, as if built yesterday, and this is equally true at the present. The tenements huddled at the rear, with their dingy walls and ravaged woodwork, seem to go much further back.

The best part of the Escorial is the basilica, domed, built in the form of a Greek cross, its proportions splendid inside and out, austere and simple without being harsh. Today, however, we could not visit it properly, as the monks were singing Mass. I would gladly have heard them out, they sang so well and looked so fine in their black and silver vestments, grave decorous sorts of men, far removed from those who once grew fat and made merry on rich harvests and full-bodied wine; but the guide raced me off in the usual tearing hurry of his profession. The one place where, like a good Spaniard, he would dally was the Panteon, the sombre vault in black and gold containing the sarcophagi of Spanish kings, with a *pudridero* each side of the entrance where royal bodies are left to rot before final interment: that on the left still holds Cristina, mother of Alfonso XII.

'I would love to get a peep at her,' he confided wistfully, 'but it is not allowed.'

There was also the tomb like a great white wedding cake, where lie a few little princes and princesses, dead before their First Communion; and the sepulchre of don Juan of Austria, with a Latin inscription below to say, 'There was a man sent from God, whose name was John,' and an effigy of the victor of Lepanto on top, with sixteen rings on his fingers in commemoration of his sixteen (known) mistresses.

Once the guide could tear himself away from these, we went round lickety-split; even so, it took us three and a half hours. Philip intended the place to be a monastery first, then the royal burial ground, then a haven of peace for himself: like other Spanish kings, he longed both to rule the world and to flee it. Those who came after turned it into an art collection and a museum as well, however, stuffing it with treasure after treasure until there was a real *embarras de richesse*. No matter how often you go, with every visit you come on priceless things never noted before. Today, one of these was the manuscript of the *Fundaciones*, which I had not even realized was here. St Teresa's generous script hurried in brown ink over the greyish vellum as she wrote in odd moments between mending a roof, comforting a novice or fighting the bishops, too hastily sometimes to finish a sentence or mind her grammar, but with a wonderful natural gift of expression. It was something to pore over at leisure, but I had hardly deciphered a couple of lines before I was bustled away. It would be so delightful to potter about unshepherded here, as in the Prado, but I never saw anyone do it: to refuse the services of a guide seems to be against all protocol.

I had luncheon in La Cueva, a folksy place with waiters in striped blouses and many bad pictures on the walls. There was also a stuffed wild cat with a little dead rabbit between its paws, a curious decoration for a dining room. It is remarkable how often restaurants in Spain have some such grisly reminder of jungle law, a stuffed eagle in the act of eating a pigeon, a picture of a dead deer with blood seeping from its mouth, or of a wild boar at bay, or of a fish struggling on a hook. Can the purpose be to whet our appetites? Or to remind us, as we eat and drink and laugh, of grim underlying realities? Or has the proprietor merely bought them in a job lot? Any of these is possible.

In the afternoon the rain stopped and the sun came out. I found a magnificent walk through a pine wood, high over the town, above the hotel Felipe II. On and on it went, the sun picking out the ridged trunks of the trees, the great rocks piled one upon the other and covered in brilliant moss. Everywhere was the spiky moroccan broom that would presently splash the earth with its cheerful yellow, and the rock rose, whose soft pink flowers die off at once in the summer heat but are replaced so fast that the shrub is perpetually covered with them. Today the prospect was unrelieved, drab and grim as the monastery and altogether in tune with it. Through a clearing came a sudden view of the tawny dome and towers, the slate-coloured roof, the sandy walls, the bleak grey stretch of water, with the Sierra behind and in between a broad wooded plain, all clear and distinct as in some old engraving. This whole walk was evidently made by man and intended for use, but there was not another soul along it, nor a scrap of litter on the ground.

Back in the town there were crumbling yellow houses with huge decaying wooden doors: the Hapsburg atmosphere prevailed despite a rash of new buildings, in the undistinguished yet unmistakable *estilo falangista*. Looking at the little square with a graceful lamp post in the centre, the granite seats, the chestnut trees around it and the old courtyards with twisted silver boughs of fig trees and brown withered vines, one could fancy oneself in a Viennese suburb, such as Grinzing. All that it lacked was Austrian gaiety. This little square, like most little squares in Spain, has been re-named Generalisimo, just that, no name, a signal honour. In a hundred years from now, perhaps, travellers may be asking, But who was this Generalisimo? And perhaps the townspeople, shocked, may answer, 'Surely you must know that?' Or perhaps, and rather more likely, they will shrug him off with a Quién sabe?

I returned to Madrid by coach: while still far off, the city lights made a sparkling pool in the darkness of the plain. The capital may seem to stagger and sprawl now, like any other industrial growth, once you are inside it: viewed from a distance at night, it remains the elegant compact little city of yore, glowing warmly under the immense black arch of the sky.

The next excursion I made was to San Martín de Valdeiglesias, and broke entirely fresh ground. It had been suggested to me some years ago by don Xavier de ——, to whom Mr Gerald Brenan had given a letter of introduction. Whether don Xavier disapproved of Mr Brenan or of myself I shall never know; but his behaviour to me was so wonderfully, wickedly, Spanish as perhaps to be worth recording.

I sent him the introduction, with a note asking if I might call. Back came the reply that he would be delighted, and giving a telephone number. I rang the number, only to hear that no one of that name lived in the house. Innocently I supposed that a secretary had made a typing error and that don Xavier had signed the letter without reading it through. I now rang up at his office, and was told that don Xavier was at present engaged but would telephone me at the first opportunity. He never did, but Irish life has accustomed me to that, and I still thought nothing of it. Now I wrote to him saying that unless he sent word to the contrary, I should like to call on such a day at such a time. No word came, and in due course I presented myself. A footman took my card into his office and returned, asking me to wait a few minutes. After forty of them had ticked slowly by, light broke in. Don Xavier, on the other side of a glass door, was clearly alone: from time to time he would ring somebody up and then go peacefully back to his work. At last he rang the bell for a footman and told him to bring me in.

'I am so sorry you were kept waiting,' he said, rising to his feet with easy grace, 'I had been called to another part of the building.'

I said I understood perfectly – by now this was true – and thanked him for his kindness in seeing me at all. He then proceeded to answer my questions and give me advice with such urbanity, I half thought my suspicions were paranoiac; but when, determined not to *molestar*, at the end of a short half hour I took my leave he produced a final shot from his locker.

'When I travel abroad,' he said, with much sweetness of manner, 'I invariably find myself short of visiting cards. No doubt you have found the same. Allow me please, before you go, to return yours to you.'

I took it, praising his thoughtfulness and alleging that I was in fact more or less cleaned out of cards; and thus, to some extent, the blow fell on space. Such methods of conveying displeasure, widely used in Spain, are known as *indirectos* and, as in this case, are about as indirect as a bullet between the eyes.

Don Xavier had urged me to visit San Martín, with special emphasis on the new *embalse*, or water catchment, a triumph, he said, of Spanish engineering; but for a long time I had put it off, half inclined to suspect that the *embalse* would prove to be one more of his little jokes. Now it occurred to me that a legpull of that kind would be every whit as instructive, to a student of Spain, as a marvel of engineering; and accordingly I resolved to go.

A bus left at half-past eight, just as day was dawning. No sooner were we off than its radio burst into cry. A notice proclaimed there was to be no singing – uncalled for, that, since no one could so much as hear himself speak. There was the usual holy image, decorated with gaudy paper flowers. From time to time the driver removed both hands from the wheel to light a cigarette or comb his hair. It was a fine drive, now through the familiar grey boulders and green umbrella pines, now over the huge undulating ribbed fields of Castille, with here and there a village crowning a hill or dropped in a hollow, and never a sign of life except for a solitary man or two on a mule.

Don Xavier had neither invented nor even exaggerated the waterworks. The Pantano de San Juan is a notable piece of engineering, for the collecting and holding of water and the generating of electricity. But it is not really for things like this that we come to Spain: we can see larger and better elsewhere. Like all developing people, the Spanish today are full of their splendid new toys and exhort the stranger to visit factories, mines and installations as if he had nothing of the kind at home.

The pueblo of San Martín itself was small and shabby and fast asleep, everything still closed up and no one astir but the emaciated dogs that snuffed about the garbage bins. The church, begun but not finished by Juan de Herrera, was woefully down at heel: a sacristan, roused from his slumbers, assured me there was nothing to see. I wanted at least to climb the tower for the sake of the view, but he would not hear of it.

'The stairs are of wood, and mostly rotten,' he declared. 'No one ever goes up there now.'

There was, as usual, no conveyance back to Madrid until the late afternoon, and a familiar sense of being trapped came over me. But the sacristan proposed a visit to the Eremita de la Nueva, where there was a minute Byzantine Virgin of great antiquity and importance: it was, he said, a stone's throw away and I should be greatly edified when I got there.

The stone's throw proved to be a full six kilometres up a steep mountain road, but the walk, once I was clear of the town, was a delightful one. First there was an *urbanización* to pass, rows of squat white villas, all exactly alike, each with a tiny garden, the mere contemplation of which brought on feelings of claustrophobia. A board announced that you could buy one of these nasty boxes in the space of a minute and take a hundred months to pay. Incredible but true! it added, in huge lettering. For the first time in Spain! But soon all this was happily left behind.

It was a stiff pull up, but the air was dry and sharp and I felt no fatigue. Not a soul was about: herds of goats or an odd mule wandered the fields alone, their neckbells jangling in plaintive chorus. Here and there was an ancient well, long used up, or a roadside chapel, domed and white-washed like a mammoth beehive. Far away on the blue horizon stupendous rock formations rose, weirdly shaped, the fantastic castles and mythical beasts of a fairy story. Below the tawny land spread out, striped with rows of vine stocks, pruned so hard they seemed no bigger than cloves, or dotted with clumps of feathery olive trees. I seemed not only to be on top of the world but, as so often in the Spanish countryside, to have it all to myself.

Once the summit was reached, the road fell steeply. On either side was a dense forest of pines, the breeze sighing patiently through their myriad branches. There were sounds of a woodman's axe and foresters calling out to each other, coming from many miles away.

Presently the Eremita came into sight, a tall squarish edifice, apparently modern. I quickened my pace, only to find it securely locked, with no chance of hunting anyone up to bring the key: why, after all these years, I had expected anything else, is difficult to imagine.

There was nothing for it but to turn back. A short distance along the road I came to a track or boreen, which I had noted on the way as apparently leading somewhere. Now I went down it, to be rewarded by something just as edifying as yet another holy doll – a magnificent mountain lake, stretching as far as the eye could see, gentian blue, glittering in the sun, with the wood falling down to its bank. Round it was what looked to be a carefully maintained park, but in fact was entirely natural, with dwarf clover and other herbs making a lawn of soft bright green and boulders lying casually about, covered with gay lichen, as if deliberately placed there for effect.

No doubt the lake eventually flowed into the reservoirs of the Pantano, and it would have been pleasant to walk along its bank so far, picking up the bus from there. But I was hungry after my early breakfast and uphill march, and, thinking there was better hope of a meal in San Martín, returned the way I had come. By now the day was warming up, and the sun drew lizards out of their holes to flicker about on the rocks. There was a sudden burst of human activity as well, a lorry passed, and a boy kicking an old tin can, two foresters called from a hut in the trees, an old man was going my way, trundling a pram heaped with firewood: evidently it was the rush hour. The fellow eagerly fastened on to me, for he was full of complaints and thirsting to pass them on; indeed, I have seldom met a more utterly dissatisfied individual.

'All this way,' he grumbled – he lived in San Martín – 'for a few logs and some kindling! I lead the life of a mule. Propio, a mule. If I were to have my time again, I should wish to be a foreigner.'

And there was much more in similar vein, about the sun, the cost of living, the neighbours and a daughter-in-law, while I fairly reeled under the fumes of garlic and decaying teeth. He went so slowly and stopped so often that presently I excused myself and went ahead: he was not offended, merely grieved at losing his audience, and he continued trumpeting his afflictions after me as long as I remained in earshot.

By the time I reached San Martín, it had come to whatever life it possessed. At the public fountain old women in black were rinsing clothes and chattering in voices like rooks or ravens. Children ran about, all smartly dressed and looking gay, and with the air that children in Spain now have of belonging to a species wholly different from their elders. The Bank had finally raised its shutters, hinting by the English, French and American flags in the window at a throng of tourists, although not one was to be seen. The restaurant, El Meson de primi los Arcos, appeared to have the same expectancy, to judge from its wrought iron and arty arrangement of dried gourds; but there were only two other guests, a commercial traveller who barked his '*Aproveche!*' on sitting down in the tones of a drill sergeant and a deaf mute, who made astounding noises over his food. Despite the meagre custom, the Meson provided an excellent meal of prawns stewed with garlic in oil, the roasted leg of a sucking lamb – one of Castille's great dishes – and iced pudding, with Cebreros rosado to drink, all for considerably less than a pound.

It had been my intention next to walk the four kilometres to the monastery of Guisando, to see the famous granite figures there known as The Bulls, although some scholars believe they are Hannibal's elephants, others, that they are primitive Iberian idols, while Ford declares they resemble nothing so much as hippopotami. They are at any rate of tremendous age, the four surviving specimens of what used to be commonly found in Castille but over the years were put by the canny natives to practical use, such as repairing roads. It was now almost four o'clock: the bus was due to leave at seven, the timetable said; and there seemed to be ample time for this improving expedition.

Man proposes, Spain disposes. As I left the Meson, the first thing to catch my eye was the blackhearted bus making its way up the road to Madrid. I broke into a run, shouting frantic appeals, in despair, weighed down by lunch as I was, of ever coming up with it. Puffing and blowing, I was about to acknowledge defeat and resign myself to another twenty-four hours in this forlorn *pueblo* when a miracle took place. It must have been a miracle because never before had I known that perverse and malevolent creature the goat do anything but what was purely destructive. A whole herd of them now tripped daintily out of a turning in front of the bus and halted there, defying all efforts to move them on until I was safely inside.

'You were nearly left behind!' the conductor observed, with a chuckle.

'I thought you left at seven,' I gasped. 'The timetable said so.'

'Timetables!' The scorn in his voice was worth hearing. 'Who pays attention to them? Always ask the people. Show me that timetable, please.' He held it up close to his eyes, his lips moving as he read. 'It must have been thinking of summer. In summer, true, we leave at seven. But this is winter, Señora, verdad?'

It is a constant mortification to me, after all my years of travelling in Spain, how often she still catches me out. Nor was the dear thing content to leave it there. In Madrid it was spilling rain once more, with the subsequent dearth of taxis. As, wet, cold and tired, I stumbled into the residencia, all the lights went off as if by prearrangement. An hour or so later they came on; but now, owing to a seismic convulsion of the plumbing system, there was no hot water. After a similar period of time, this service too was restored: I was just stepping thankfully into the bath when the lights went off again.

Ah, don Xavier, don Xavier . . .

I set off for Segovia at seven o'clock on the cold and frosty morning of December 8th. The demon who supervises travel in Spain had prompted me to choose that day, it being the feast of the Immaculate Conception, when the country more or less grinds to a standstill. There would be no coach, said the booking-clerk in triumph, when I appeared the evening before to reserve a place on it; and now I was rattling through the dark deserted streets to catch the only train.

In making journeys here, the prudent habits of a lifetime are best discarded. Having arrived at the station with several minutes to spare, I found myself, as so often before, completely alone. Everything was shut, with a sardonic air of intending to remain so. Some way off up the line was a magnificent timber fire with workmen round it, talking, their faces lit by the leaping red flames: apart from their voices and the whistle of the wind, all was silent and dead.

Half an hour after the train should have left, the passengers began strolling up in twos and threes. They were mostly young, dressed for the mountains and looking a little odd, as Spaniards in sporting attire are apt to do. Presently a light shone in the ticket office and the hatch opened, and we made a rush for it as if there were no time to lose, although the train was not even signalled. Finally the ticket collector appeared, yawning, and dreamily punched our tickets.

'We shall be somewhat behindhand today,' he prophesied.

The holiday-makers showed neither resentment nor impatience, but stood in serried ranks, leaning on their skis, their faces blue with cold, their heads turned hopefully in the direction whence the train should come; and at last, when we were all but frozen stiff, come it did.

The line ran straight to the Guadarrama, passing the Valley of the Fallen with its simple tremendous cross, and entered the first of the tunnels. In Madrid the frost was hard and black but now, as we shot out into daylight again, we were all of a sudden in snow country. At Navacerrada the sportsmen, blithe and garrulous, jumped out and dashed for the funicular to the peaks. Then on to Cudillos and El Espinar, and the sun appeared in a lovelyy turquoise sky, with little dove-coloured clouds drifting across it, over the huge Segovian plain, dazzling white, with here and there the dark shapes of cattle, rocks or pines, or a stream running black between heavy fringes of scrub.

At Segovia, a bus was waiting to bring us into the town, the station being, as Spanish stations so often are, built a couple of miles outside. I shared an exiguous seat with an enormous but friendly woman, whose voice rode easily above the roar of the engine as she put me through the customary inquisition. The aqueduct loomed up ahead, the tremendous arches grimy against the snow. As soon as the bus halted, I tumbled out, frozen to the marrow, and scuttled into the nearest *churrería*. It was a smoky little den that, with its charcoal burners, bulging sacks and piles of brushwood, seemed to belong to another age. A youth stood by the fire, squeezing what looked like a pair of bellows, from which dough went ribboning into a cauldron of sizzling fat and was fried in a matter of seconds. This he then fished out and divided with a pair of medieval shears, offering me a number of lengths in one of his black and greasy paws. The proprietor, squat, lowbrowed and with a cast in one small eye, poured liquid from a rusty kettle and pushed it over the counter without a word. It did not look or taste like coffee,

51

but was evidently intended as such; and he asked a fancy price for it, and gave me back short change.

All these things in their different ways helped to promote the circulation. Feeling restored, I went on to the Bar Castilla which, in honour of La Purísima, was already quite full. At the far end, countrymen in black berets and corduroys were drinking beakers of wine, smoking, playing cards and spitting on the floor: the near was occupied by the bourgeoisie, sedately reading their papers and drinking coffee. The invigorating buzz of Castilian thrummed on my ear. I took a seat and hissed at the bootblack, nodding on a chair by the window. He came forward and drowsily brushed, creamed, polished and fondled my tall Italian boots until they were the rich oily black of his own gipsy hair.

'This should last you for a while,' he said languidly. 'It is rare to find me at work these days.' And off he went to resume his nap.

Presently above the general buzz there rose a specific uproar. A card-player was offering to fight another, who had impugned his probity. He had leaped up and thrown aside his coat, and now was struggling in the grip of friends, who had seized and held him in the traditional way.

'Let me go! Let me get at him!'

'Hombre! not in here!'

'Outside, then! Fuera! Vamos!'

He continued fiercely struggling, as etiquette demanded, while the waiters looked on with the unconcern of experience, until the whole affair died down as suddenly as it had started up, the cards were dealt afresh and the game went peacefully forward.

More time-honoured ritual was waiting at the hotel Las Sirenas, further up the narrow busy Calle de Cervantes. Well knowing that at this season it would be all but empty, I had not bothered to make a reservation and watched, with the appreciation of a connoisseur, the pantomime that followed. Frowning portentously, the concierge studied the register for a while, then

shrugged his shoulders and sadly shook his head.
'Impossible!' he said. 'We are quite full.'

My move.

'I was afraid you would be. It is only natural. Where do you suggest I could try?'

'Really, I don't know. Segovia is very full at present.'

'Well, may I leave this suitcase here while I look round?'

'Certainly, with pleasure.'

I was barely fifty yards from the door when a diminutive Buttons came flying after me. 'Tssst! Señora! Please come back.'

Now the concierge was wreathed in smiles. 'What a lucky coincidence!' he exclaimed. 'Just as you went out, a gentleman rang down to say he would be leaving. Please make your paseo, Señora, and enjoy it. The room shall be prepared meanwhile.'

It turned out later that, for the moment, I was the only guest.

With things so pleasantly arranged, I went for a walk round the lovely old town, which I had never before seen under snow. Its beauty in winter dress quite took the breath away, with snow-covered trees, roofs, statues and fountains all sparkling in the sun, walls of the Cathedral, Alcazar, churches and ancient houses a warm yellow against the deep blue of the sky. It must be one of the least spoiled of Spanish cities. New industries are springing up in the countryside around, and there is a certain amount of development in the lower districts that spill out over the plain, but the whole upper region, covering a hill, with the Cathedral as its crown, is quite untouched, as if declared a National Monument in its entirety and forever; and for all the different styles, Roman, Gothic, Mudejar, even baroque, it blends into a harmonious whole, with nothing that jars anywhere.

If it was beautiful in the sunny forenoon, at evening when darkness fell, it was entrancing. Accustomed to the street-lights of the present day, their hideous mouths fixed in a cold blue grin, I had forgotten the allure of old iron lamps, delicately wrought, that shed their pools of soft yellow light in mysterious shadows around. Tonight, in honour of the Virgin, various points were illumined, which more than made up for the earlier discomforts of the day. The aqueduct, bestriding the lower end of the city, was stupendous. Two thousand years old, doubtless good for two thousand more, the greatest Roman survival in Spain, the stones laid one upon the other so artfully as to need no cementing, it is a marvel seen under any conditions. But now columns and arches that in sunlight had looked so drab against the snow were the colour of honey: high up the gold and crimson of Spain fluttered round the little Madonna, secure in the niche from which she had ousted Hercules; and the sense one had of its power and calm and abiding majesty, with the starry sky above and the chattering crowds below, was overwhelming. Spanish historians tell us with pride that Celtic resistance to the Roman invader was particularly furious in these parts; but they should rather give thanks that it failed, for Celts have never been good for much except resisting, and their legacy would hardly have been of a kind to draw the crowds.

As I wandered on and on through narrow cobbled lanes, all at once I would come on a familiar church, palace or tower magically given a new face, by means of this floodlighting, perfectly used. The little *plazas* that are a Segovian feature were exquisite, shrubs and bushes heavy with snow and sparkling under the lamps, stonework glittering with long sharp tongues of ice. The *plazita* named for Dr Andrés de Laguna, 1499-1559, Poet, Orator, Diplomat, Creator of the first botanical garden at Aranjuez, and of course a Son of Segovia, was particularly splendid, with the Doctor himself, lean, long-nosed, vague and bookish, all lit up as if he had been the Lady of Elche herself, on a lawn that flashed like a carpet of diamonds, ringed about with ghostly trees.

'Guapo, no?' asked a jovial passer-by.

'Guapísimo. But who,' I inquired, 'was he?' The question was frivolous, since I already knew, but I expected some amusement from his reply.

'Who can tell? A man of olden times.' That much could
have been inferred from the long medieval robes; and the
list of his attributes, carved on the pedestal in clear bold lettering, could almost have been a pointer too. 'But guapo.'

The citizen appeared to consider that this was enough.
To my next question, however, he replied in full, without
hesitation.

'Why isn't the Cathedral floodlit as well? Money. Not
enough to go round. The aqueduct comes first. Anyone can
have a cathedral.'

A little further on in the Plaza Mayor, an evening *paseo* of
young people was in progress. The last time I had seen this
here was in high summer and it was still conducted in the
traditional way. Round and round they paced, the girls in
one direction, the boys in the other, past the Cathedral,
through the arcades, under the plane trees, laughing and
talking. The boys murmured *piropos* or compliments in the
ears of young women that took their fancy and the girls put
their noses in the air, pretending not to know that such
things as boys existed. Now all that was changed. Bands of
girls pelted along shrieking at the top of their lungs, hotly
pursued by boys, yelling and whooping like Indians, and
vigorously snowballed. Here and there a tipsy lad was
helped along by friends, another novelty and further witness to the country's transformation. I had long ago concluded that the sober frugal Spaniard was a myth and that
the poor devil had merely been hard up; but I had never
seen a rustic Spanish boy under the weather before, and
these unsteady little figures made some impression.

Manners of both the sexes had changed as well and, tired
of being jostled and pushed and jeered at for a Frenchie, I
walked down to the Peñal on Cervantes for a glass of wine.
It was crowded, with many unescorted women in the
throng. At one table there were six of them, middle-aged,
clinking with cheap jewellery, their dyed hair combed in
the *bouffant* Spanish way that makes the head look abnor-
mally large, and, literally, all talking at once. Everyone was
spending freely, and there were people treating themselves

55

to the various shellfish, one of Spain's most expensive delicacies, who, a few years before, could hardly have indulged in more than a cana of cheap wine. Someone had chalked the words GIGANTIC OYSTERS TODAY! ! ! on the wall, presumably in the belief that size and excellence were one. I ordered a few of the smaller kind that have more taste, which led to an argument with the waiter; but I held my ground and very delicious they were, fresh and tangy as the sea itself for all they had come by road from La Coruña.

By now the whole city was making merry in tribute to the immaculate conception of the Mother of God. The cafés, bars, restaurants and taverns were crammed, and strident music poured out to the world whenever a door was opened. For dinner I went to the Meson de Candido, an excellent if rather self-conscious it keeps a Golden Book to be signed by the noble, rich or famous, who presumably reveal their identities on arrival. The maître d'hôtel ran to and fro, presenting the customers with flowers and wine jugs to take away. Waiters bustled about with huge portions of Castilian dishes. Sucking-pigs lay like roasted babies on the platters, their little faces wearing a look of indignant surprise. There were whole legs of sucking lamb, fat capons neatly split in two, plump trout from the local rivers, earthenware jugs of regional wine, ornate loaves of crusty bread: merely to contemplate these mountains of food was almost in itself a meal.

All the diners were Spanish, mainly of the new rich, eating away as if determined to make up for centuries of famine. Two women, heavily painted and with rows of bracelets on either wrist, greeted each course with little cries of genteel dismay before falling upon it with a zest delightful to see, drawing their soup in hloop hloop hloop, gnawing bones to the ultimate scrap of gristle and scouring their plates with bread until they shone. A solitary man with four or five chins and diamonds sparkling on several fingers munched course after course, emptied jug upon jug and, still in good heart, wound up with the elaborate dessert known as Virgin's Peak, looking on with the gravity of a child as the waiter flamed its snowy, sugary slopes.

My own meal was of asparagus, chicken and the famous Segovian cake called *ponche*, meaning punch, although the English leaflet from Turismo called it grog. It was a delicate biscuity affair with layers of marzipan and candied yolk of egg, steeped in rum and much too sickly for me; but the Marqués de Lozoya had described it in his book on the region as 'the best rounding-off to a day of art'. He also remarked that in general the sweetmeats of Segovia, 'as in all cities of quiet life', were excellent, but with a reservation. The recipes of them all were of ancient and venerable monastic origin: at the beginning of the century, each of the ten or twelve convents in the city had its own particularly famous one, passed on by the generations, from nun to novice, and bestowed on the privileged at Christmas, Easter and birthday; and the purity of their raw materials and the care they took in the preparation resulted in quality beyond the reach of worldly tradesmen.

'Candy egg-yolk of Las Dominicas!' the noble gourmet cries, 'Shortcake of San Antonio el Real! Soaked biscuit of Santa Isabel! Almond flan of Las Peraltas! With the memory of your vanished glories, which sweetened my childhood, I will end this brief account of things Segovian. For the palate, too, has its powerful capacity for evocation.'

And after that, I could hardly do less than sample the grog.

Leaving, I had to pass an outer bar and here fell into the hands of three incoherent revellers who would not allow me to proceed until we had all drunk together. One of them, unshakeably convinced that General de Gaulle had been Prime Minister of England, plied me with intimate questions about him and was gravely disappointed by my lack of information. Another was most insistent that I should come for a *gira* in his motor-car, and *gira* would just about have been the word for it, as the honest fellow was gyrating already on his own two feet. With many polite regrets I slipped away and up the hill to Las Sirenas, where the diminutive Botones, feasting his eyes on the *muchadumbre* in the street, opened the door for me with an inelegant kick and said good night with a dreamy wave of the hand.

Segovia was still keeping it up when I went to bed after midnight, and I was hardly asleep before a caterwauling under the window roused me again. Someone was attempting to sing *flamenco*, which Castilian drunks are fond of doing, and with the usual lack of success, while soberer companions reproved him. Presently he lifted up his voice and, loud and clear, sang two lines of the Red Flag. Anxious for a peep at so intrepid or desperate a character, I ran to the window, in time to see his friends throw a coat over his head and pull him struggling away. Then all at last was peace, broken only by the chime of a clock or the distant bark of a dog, while the stars glittered in the frosty night and the broad rolling plain beyond the city lay buried as far as the eye could see under deep crisp snow.

Next morning I was to have been called at half past seven, in time for Mass at the papal convent of San José, founded by Teresa of Avila. Luckily I woke up of myself, for nothing whatever happened; and, on coming downstairs, I found the night porter merrily playing cards with some friends. No one, he said, had asked him to give the call; to whom had the message been entrusted? I said it was to the little page, whereat all four men shouted 'Botones!' in chorus and with great relief, as if things were now fully explained. It appeared that he was so busy making money on the side as to have no time for his duties. For the moment I was somewhat vexed, but before I left Segovia I had grown quite fond of this original if useless little character.

The only other person at Mass was a jolly woman, who acted as the convent caretaker. The nuns were hidden behind their grille, their responses sweet and trenchant, as if a bush full of blackbirds were taking part. The church was in darkness except for three candles on the altar, lighting up the *retablo* of heavy dull gold with its vine leaf pattern and figure of St Joseph with the Child; and the priest threw great flickering shadows on the walls as he moved silently to and fro, with a strange and eerie effect.

The priest had noted my presence, however, and the minute mass was done sent an acolyte to tell the caretaker the lights must be switched on, so that the church could be properly seen. On the whole, darkness suited it better; but I enjoyed listening to the woman, who chatted freely about the nuns – 'twenty of them, all very pleasant' – and about the Foundress herself, as if she had died only the other day. She told me she herself lived *sola sola* in a little room near by and ran the messages, did the shopping and saw to everything connected with the outside world: it was not an arduous life, as the nuns ate very little and always fish, fish, fish.

It was still dark and freezing cold when I left the church. I had a fancy for a cup of chocolate and walked over half Segovia trying to get a cup of what, after all, is Spain's own breakfast drink, but to no avail. In the Meson de Candido, a barman with moustaches like a Mexican bandit assured me that no one had ever asked for such a thing before.

'Is that what you drink in your own country?' he asked. 'No? Then why drink it here?'

By now the sun was rising, and it was clear that we should have another magnificent day. I went through the streets, orderly and workaday once again, to the Puerta de Santiago, where the road abruptly changed to an earthen track, as if what happened beyond the city wall was of no importance. This track was planted with handsome trees, and a woman was going from one to the other with a washing-line, searching for a pair close enough together to take it: a hopeless task, it appeared, but Spanish municipal trees are not always evenly spaced and when I came back later on she had the family wash hanging out, pants, shirts, nightdresses, aprons in all sizes and colours, a homelike touch in these grave historic surroundings.

The track descended, winding, to a bridge across the Eresma, more stream than river, but brimming over at this time of year and muttering to itself as it hurried along. On one of its banks stood the Sanctuary of Our Lady of the Fuencisla, patroness of Segovia, beautifully placed before a pinky orange cliff with martens wheeling about its towers. Inside it was dull and dusty, with a few votive candles flickering in the draught and no sign of life at all. In front was a little bosky, charming for summer picnics, and a kiosk shut for the winter but flaunting the badge of Coca Cola.

An old peasant rode up with heavy clay pots slung over his mule's back and began to fill them at a fountain near by. The *burro* serenely drank as well in spite of a notice which forbade him, his owner remarking with a wide toothless smile that the poor brute had never learned to read. 'We did our best, but his heart wasn't in it,' he told me. He chatted as the pots were filling, putting none of the usual questions about myself but making pithy observations on the state of the world, which he saw as one of decline; and broke off the instant his jars were full, clambered on the heavily laden beast and went about his affairs, humming as gaily as a boy.

Not far off was the monastery of St John of the Cross, where that wonderful man, one of the most appealing figures of Spanish history, is buried. I rang the bell, again and again, and in something like half an hour a friar pushed the grille back and smiled a welcome through it. The order being enclosed, he bade me wait in the church, where he soon appeared, a man of thirty or so, who might have been a contemporary of the saint, with his laughing eyes, hollow cheeks and stubbly chin, his old brown habit and worn sandals. Swinging a bunch of keys he led the way to the relics, clearly supposing them to be one of the chief attractions; but he bustled along at such a speed that I hardly took them in, and only remember the saint's elaborate diagram of the Way to Perfection (*conviviencia*) by means of prayer, from which it was possible to conclude that he was a better poet than draughtsman. The church was commonplace, even tawdry, and not kept up very well, the one point of real interest being the chapel in which St John is lying. Under the floor is the grave he occupied at first: a trap-door opens on a narrow shaft descending to the rough stone crypt beneath. This surely is what the saint would have preferred, but they had him out of it and into an urn on the top of a massive pedestal, ornate but unsightly, with carvings of angels, apostles and other VIPs all round it. From time to time they opened the coffin to see how things were going, the last occasion having been in 1955.

'Still uncorrupt,' the friar remarked with satisfaction, 'Think of it! after nearly four centuries.'

It was a little puzzling because over and over again in Teresian foundations one of the most cherished of all the relics will be a bone from St John's body; but it was not the moment to make difficulties, with the friar gazing on the tomb in such love and pride. I assured him I would never forget the sight of it and offered a *limosna*, which he slipped into his pocket without looking to see how much it was, promised that God would pay it back and left me with a farewell wave of his keys.

Further on was the Church of the True Cross, founded by the Knights Templar in 1208. For better or worse this enchanting piece of Romanesque has been declared a national monument: now we buy a ticket from the *custode* instead of giving alms to a friar, which is cheaper but not as human. The arrangement and the lighting are in excellent taste, and all gewgaws have been cleared out: little is left but the wonderful thirteenth century Christ Crucified of wood, a figure not dropping in agony but poised lightly as a dancer and with serenity in every line of feature and body. But for all the care lavished upon it, the place was chilly, forsaken, dead, where the Carmelite church, despite its vulgarity, was alive and warm and inhabited: it is what we have to expect when the Bellas Artes move in. They had also laid hands on the monastery of Parral, the great Gothic abbey over the hill, beautifully placed beside the river bustling past to a foaming weir and lined with poplar trees, while a few decaying cottages huddled near the bridge like Lazarus at the rich man's gate. Lorries were drawn up in the courtyard, a fierce hammering came from within and there was a notice to say that the *donativo* was five pesetas. The monk who answered the bell, however, seemed to consider the arrangement beneath him, for he waved my money away. He was a pleasant, rather melancholy man, who looked as if he rarely ate or slept, and he only spoke if a question were put to him: he told me with a sigh that a mere fifteen monks remained in the monastery now. No doubt the community will dwindle year by year inside their crumbling yellow walls until all are gone and another museum is added to the *patrimonio nacional*. But the monastery was an impressive sight today, glowing in the winter sun, and from the brow of the hill above there was a view of all Segovia, dominated by the Cathedral and with the dazzling peaks of the sierras for a background.

I now walked the two kilometres or so to the little *pueblo* of Zamarramala, perched on a hill just level with the parapet of the Alcazar, so that there was a splendid view of that castle across the valley between, looking more like an ogre's keep than ever against the snow.

To see that view had been the object of my walk; but, once there, I remembered that the *pueblo* was noted for a curious fiesta on the fifth of January, when the women take command of the place, levying fines on the men and subjecting them to all kinds of indignities. There was a knot of women in the market-place, sturdily built creatures who looked as if they really might be in the saddle the whole year round, and who burst out laughing when I inquired about their custom.

'Are you married?' asked one. 'No? Then go and get yourself a husband, and perhaps we'll tell you.'

This gave rise to more laughter, and ribaldries came flying thick and fast. After a while, however, the good souls relented and told me to call on the bakeress, as she was an expert. I did so, and found a pleasant woman of forty-odd with floury hands, who burst into a spate of talk there was no damming. The antimasculine side of things appeared to interest her least, or perhaps she felt shy of discussing it with a stranger; but she had much to say of the *fiesta* itself, centuries and centuries old, with religious observances, a great banquet – the only man present being the Señor Cura – music and dancing, and everyone in regional dress. Two *alcaldesas*, or mayoresses, were elected every year, always different, who had to be wives or widows, but needed no other qualification and had no duties at all for the rest of the year. Their task was to lead the ceremonies on the day, and to collect the fines, dues and other exactions from the men, to be applied to the cost of the party. Fifteen years ago she had been one of the chosen; and she now produced a large coloured photograph of herself in a beautiful Segovian skirt, embroidered in red and black, with an elaborate head-dress and white shawl, and the Alcazar in the distance.

'Would you have known this was I?' she demanded, smiling without a trace of coquetry. I assured her, she looked not a day older. She talked on and on until at last I tore myself away, to find that the lunch-time bus back to Segovia was a figment of the bus company's imagination, and that a long cold walk awaited me instead.

Subsequent attempts to discover the origin of the feast came to naught, for the male authorities I consulted kept as mum as the bakeress. The Marqués de Lozoya's book gave a full account of the junketings, but said 'the antecedents of this most ancient tradition lose themselves in the dawnings of history.' Don Mariano Grau, the official *cronista*, who knows his region inside out, merely smiled and gave me a leaflet, in which the frolics were described yet again. The strange thing was, the *fiesta* was held in honour of St Agueda, martyred in 251, and distinguished by her humility. 'I am a servant of Christ,' she told the Governor of Sicily, who reproached her, as member of an illustrious family, for consorting with slaves, 'and therefore of servile condition.' And again, 'The true nobility is to be Christ's slave.' None of this sounds much like Women's Lib, and in fact the saint is chiefly known as a quencher of fires: after her torture by red hot irons, this was an appropriate occupation, and she has frequently calmed the rage of Etna itself. Nevertheless, in 1227, the modest Sicilian girl somehow landed in Zamarramala, there to preside over fiery Segovian matrons whose activities she must secretly deplore.

In the afternoon I drove out to the Convent of San Antonia el Real, a magnificent pile surrounded by elm trees

64

in a down-at-heel quarter on the southern edge of the city. It was founded as a *casa de placer* in 1455 by the prince who later became Henry IV, when his father John II appointed him lord of Segovia; but on his succession he made it over to the Franciscans, who were followed in turn by Clarisas during the reign of the Catholic Kings. I was taken round by two tiny brown nuns who had a dispensation from *clausura* to receive visitors and talk to them. There were only twenty-one of them in the community now, discalced like those in Madrid, but with a most important difference too, for those in Madrid were part of the *patrimonio nacional*, whereas 'we may be poor, but all this is ours.' And very fine it all was, the church to begin with and then the *clausura* whose splendid Mudejar ceilings, a legacy of the brief but beneficent Moorish rule, were good as new, so good I asked if they had been restored.

'Not a bit of it, we couldn't restore anything, for we are much too poor, and anyhow they have never needed it,' said the smaller of the two little nuns, who took the lead.

Certainly they seemed poor enough, compared with the sister house in Madrid: perhaps they never had treasures or perhaps they had sold them one by one in time of need. Apart from the great Flemish altar-piece in the church, said to be the best of its kind in Europe, there was little of artistic value. Curiosities and relics abounded, a St Francis carved from the trunk of a tree, an array of parchments in the king's own room, paintings with stories behind them, articles of furniture used by the royal family. In one glass case there was an MS of the Gloriana, and the nuns urged me to sing it from the notes, which I tried to do, as I thought with no little success, until a stifled sound made me turn to see the fatter, less talkative nun sitting in the king's chair and rocking with helpless laughter. On the wall were frescoes, damaged almost beyond recognition: their seediness and the noble proportions of the room itself made a contrast that was truly Spanish.

The nuns said I could not leave without visiting their garden, and we took a turn in it together. They must have wanted a breath of air themselves, as the plot was narrow and featureless, entirely covered in snow. One of them stopped and scrabbled in it like a terrier after a rat, until she came on a few dejected pansies, which she plucked and offered to me. A startled cry burst from the other as a work-man appeared on the roof, whistling gaily and unslinging his bag of tools; and we hastened indoors, the nuns mutter-ing to each other in agitation, as if they had been trapped into committing a mortal sin. Now they shyly led me to a stall of modest souvenirs, where I bought some lace hand-kerchiefs made in the convent: they brightened charmingly at this and both began talking together, wishing me all manner of nice things as well as a safe journey. Like many cloistered nuns, they had an absurd, almost crazy, idea of the perils lurking beyond their convent wall.

'And nothing happens to you? Travelling about all alone?'

'In Spain? Is it likely?'

'Yes, but all those coaches and trains! And aeroplanes, por Dios! How about accidents?'

'That is as God wishes.'

'Of course, that is so; but do you not take precautions as well? Do you, for instance, not recommend yourself to St Raphael?'

'I thought it was St Christopher.'

'Certainly he is all right too, for cars and things; but for people travelling in general, St Raphael is the man.'

And, as they left me at the gate, they stole timid glances at the world outside, as if half expecting a demon to spring up and bear me away.

There is a peculiar charm about Spanish convents, at any rate in such brief glimpses of their life as the worldling man-ages to get. They have a flavour all their own, not medieval so much as timeless, and an innocence that frequently verges on the singular. That evening, after a stroll through the ancient Jews' quarter behind the Cathedral, I turned in at the Convent of Corpus Christi and rang the bell beside the revolving hatch. A gentle voice gave the customary greeting: Ave Maria Purísima. I told the invisible speaker that here was a foreigner, anxious to learn about the Jewish sacrilege and subsequent miracle that took place on this spot in 1410. 'Please wait,' she said, 'and I will get you a full account of it.' After a few moments, the hatch swivelled creakily round, bringing a small printed booklet, which I took, leaving a bank note in its place and spinning the hatch again.

'Thank you, that is very acceptable,' said the nun. 'And you will be greatly edified by what you read.'

Edified was not the word, perhaps: I could hardly believe my eyes. In 1410 a sacristan of the church of San Facundo, worried by a debt which, under pain of excommunication, he had to settle within a certain time, determined to ask a money-lending Jewish doctor for an advance. 'Friend,' quoth the Jew, 'I will give you it, and much more, if you will bring me the Body of Christ, called by your people God.' The sacristan agreed and brought him the Host, which the Jew seized in his dirty hands (*con sus manos sucias*) and ran with it to the synagogue. There, in the presence of other rejoicing Jews, he set a cauldron of resin to boil, intending to throw into it the Body of Our Saviour Jesus. But see the great mystery of the sacred Host! It simply flew round and round in the air, with the wicked men trying to catch it, while the whole synagogue shook to its foundations and the air was filled with a mighty roaring. Appalled, the Jews now took a clean cloth, wrapped the Host therein, and brought it to the monastery of the Holy Cross, where they recounted the event to the Prior after swearing him to secrecy. The Prior, together with the community, carried the Host to the altar in high pomp and state. Now at that time there was a certain novice called Espinar, who had been falling away in his life and morals. The Prior determined to administer the Host to this backslider who, three days afterwards, died gloriously in a state of grace, and, seeing so great a miracle, the Prior deemed it wrong to hide it or to honour his vow of silence.

All this, amazingly, the convent was still handing out as

literally, historically, true. From that point on, however, the most sceptical person alive can safely believe every word. The chronicler recounts the castigation of the Jews, particularly of the money-lending doctor, who confessed in torment to many other crimes, including the poisoning of King Henry (II); for which first he, and then his accomplices, were dragged through the streets behind a town crier and presently quartered. Justice done, the Bishop and clergy went in solemn procession to the site of the miracle and consecrated it for the Church of Corpus Christi, standing there to this day. Nor did the Bishop leave it at that, or cease from his inquisitions. Now some of the Jews, in dread, resolved to kill him off and, bribing their way into his kitchen, mixed poison into a sauce. But a cook happened to taste it in time and gave the alarm: the Jews were seized and tortured, some being afterwards burned, some drawn and quartered, others less guilty, garrotted or banished for ever. The pious writer ends his work with a fervent *Laus Deo*!

It is amusing, if futile, to wonder what really lay behind legends such as these. Did the Bishop's eye, one day, chance to fall on the synagogue and did he bethink him, here was the very site for that new foundation he was planning? Did everything else follow on from there? It would accord all too well with medieval church practice. I decided to visit the public library, a fine patrician building just over the way from Las Sirenas, and consult don Julio Baroja's monumental work on the Jews in Spain, for don Julio has a fairly brisk way with the marvellous.

When I got to the library, however, I found it quite packed out, with not a vacant place to be had. This was astounding, for Spaniards are not great readers, and more astounding yet, these bookworms were all remarkably young. But after watching them for a while, I realized the explanation. They were school-children, availing themselves of the light, warmth and comfort of the room to do their homework there. The librarians were acting as ushers, pacing up and down and urging quiet as the children giggled and whispered and passed their little notes. It was a human and sensible arrangement, but something of a hindrance to those in pursuit of knowledge.

7

That night a thaw set in, and the day broke in mildness and mist. Every particle of snow had vanished and the trees looked fresh, as if spring were already here. Now there was colour on all sides, more so than in summer, when the ferocious light burns the land to a deathly pale. East of the city, the tawny earth rolled away as far as the eye could see, with sandy roads and tracks snaking across it: to the west were low green hills dotted with umbrella pines, natural terraces of yellow rock with the dark mouth of a cave yawning here and there, against a frame of snowy peaks on the horizon. Towards the end of the Calle Velarde, which leads to the Alcazar, was a house with a plaque saying, Here lived Maurice Fromkes, American painter, in love with (*enamorado de*) the land of Segovia. That was something not at all hard to believe.

Velarde was one of two local captains of artillery, who fell heroically on that great Second of May 1808, fighting the French. There was a monument to them in front of the Alcazar itself, which I stopped to examine; and a wonderfully Spanish job it was, both in conception – it shows the two lads dying in the arms of Spain – and in execution, for it was decreed by the Cortes in 1812 and constructed only in 1908.

It was not for the monument's sake that I was there, striking as it might be. I was looking for the house of Antonio Machado, the great poet who sang the grandeurs and beauties of Castille as no other has done, although himself a native of Andalusia. The address in my guidebook was Vallejo 2, and thither I had gone, or tried to go, for no such place existed. Having inquired of various citizens without avail, I approached a policeman, who thought he remembered hearing the name. But, he said, better to go down to the Plaza del Azoguejo beyond the aqueduct and ask his colleague on point duty there, as he was a specialist in *turismo*. The colleague left the traffic to mind itself while, groaning and wrinkling his brow, he pondered the matter. 'Go on up to the Plaza Mayor,' he said at last. 'Someone there will tell you.' No one did, but a man suggested I consult the *custode* at the portals of the Alcazar, why, he did not say and the *custode* could not imagine. Having walked some four or five miles by now, I was on the point of giving up, as so often before; and I was wandering vaguely along when I stumbled on the house by chance in the Calle de los Desamparados, a bust of the poet in the small neat garden of which being my only clue. Accident, as Ford so truly remarks, is the moving power of things in Spain.

At the top of some old dusty stairs was the flat, whose bell I rang. A woman answered, took a look at me and called out, 'Mother! Someone for don Antonio.' A little old woman with white hair and gentle dignified manners came out, walking with difficulty, and showed me to the tiny room where Machado had lived and worked, with an old-fashioned iron bedstead, a small table and uncomfortable chair, tin washing basin and jug, and a rickety casement window looking over a number of shabby tiled roofs to the wide Castilian plain. Reverently preserved as well was a pestilential oil-stove, which had all but choked the poet and did not warm him, and the iron pot wherein, endlessly smoking, he dropped his ash. The house had taken boarders cheaply, and the old lady had been its proprietor: she spoke of her great lodger with affection and amusement. 'Goodness, the mountains of paper the man used up!' Here he spent thirteen years, teaching French in the Instituto General y Technico, and, after his death, friends acquired the house and maintained it. There was a handsome visitors' book, which doña Luisa politely asked me to sign. Among others to do so, was one of those strange Americans who can never put their names without adding strings of verse, deeply felt and tritely conceived, by themselves: this particular masterpiece, I remember, led off with the words, 'And did you have to die, Machado?'

The memory of that small bare room stays sharp and clear. There was something in it, as in Machado's frugal way of life, that seemed to accord with the grave powerful resonances of his work. For him, there was neither the misery of a Verlaine nor the ease and comfort of a Tennyson, but a simple quiet round of duty gaining him the leisure to write his poems. In one of them he reminds the world, without bitterness, that while it owes him all he has produced he owes it nothing whatever, has always earned his bread and paid his way. For recreation, he had the talk of friends in tertulias at the café, or long solitary walks through the harsh beloved countryside or the decrepit towns of Castille, walks on which he conversed with the man who always accompanied him (*converso con el hombre que siempre va conmigo*), in other words, himself.

Appropriately, my next call was on a distinguished local character who had known Machado well as a boy. This was don Mariano Grau, the *cronista*, who sat in the Town Hall assisting those in need of advice or information with a delightful lack of ceremony. I had already been to see him once and was shown in directly, against all Spanish custom. The open door he kept may well have been due to the influence of Machado, for in a charming memoir of the poet he records how, with youthful egotism, he visited him every day and carried him off for a walk, even reciting to him the 'versos horrendos' he had composed himself, and never once was snubbed or treated with anything but affable patience; and how this continued until a candid friend reproved him for wasting Machado's precious time and being a *molestia*, on which he was seized with shame and remorse and never went near his idol again.

72

At the Town Hall, a messenger led me through draughty passages with dire contemporary pictures on the walls to don Mariano's office, a den filled almost to capacity by his one chair and a table strewn with documents. The *cronista* jumped up as I appeared and hurried me off to a handsome conference room with a long table and high-backed chairs. He was a big lively man with a keen sense of humour, and he smoked one cigarette after another, like most Spaniards who can afford to do so. I told him that, glorious and unequalled as Segovia's antiquities were, I should now like to see something a little more of the moment; and he immediately launched into what appeared to be a set piece. He spoke of the great improvement in Segovia whose industry, once the finest in Spain and perhaps in Europe, was now rising after a decadence lasting for centuries. New factories opened all the time, and indeed DYC, one of the two Spanish whiskies, was 'fabricated' only four kilometres away. I really should visit the factory, for it was thoroughly up-to-date and a going concern. He would introduce me to the Mayor, who was on the board, and the Mayor would tell the manager to expect me. With that, he leaped to his feet again; but when we got to the Mayor's office, that dignitary was not to be found. Don Mariano installed me in another conference room, even more magnificent than the first, although most of the chairs were shrouded in dust-covers and there was a pile of washing on the sofa.

While we waited I endeavoured to draw don Mariano out, with no success whatever. He was voluble and amusing as long as he held forth on a theme of his own, but let me only put a question, however harmless, and he at once became cautious and monosyllabic, as if wondering what I was really after. One thing I did gather was that no problems of any kind existed in the Spain of today, and that everything was as rosy as it could be. Presently someone put his head round the door and said the Mayor was back. We moved to the anteroom outside his office and waited half an hour or so, watching anxious little men scurry in and out with their files, all smoking away like mad. At last we were admitted to the mayoral presence, and our business settled in a matter of seconds.

'I shall ring the factory and tell them you will come this afternoon,' the Mayor said, bowing over my hand with courtly grace. 'All you need do is call a taxi and just say whisky! to the driver.'

This proved to be exact. Pepe, the old rascal I employed whenever I could, gave a prodigiously knowing wink and whirled me off to the distillery without further ado.

It was not like business premises at all, but a most attractive place with lawns, flowerbeds, willow trees and ponds, well-kept and homely like the *bodegas* at Jerez de la Frontera. The main building, once a convent, was old and handsome, while a newer one beside it had plainly been inspired by the Escorial. A smart good-looking boy took me round, explaining all the different procedures and equipment with manifest pride until we came at the last to the bottling shed. Now there was nothing for it but to accept a glassful of the product. It was extraordinary, so much so that I am puzzled how to describe it. It seemed to have been made by people who had perhaps read up the subject of whisky and its distillation, but had not actually tasted any and had only a vague idea of what they were trying to do. There was a curious underlying flavour of Spanish brandy in it, and a hot prickly rawness, as with surgical spirit or disinfectant.

'Is it as good as your Scotch?' the boy asked, somewhat anxiously.

I replied that, in its own way, it surely was but that it was also different.

'But do you like it as well?' he persisted.

'Well . . . as a rule we leave whisky to itself a while before we drink it.'

'We too!' he cried, glad of this point in common. 'We never sell a drop under three years old.'

I asked him if it was the only Spanish whisky, and he said no, there was another *fabrica* in Barcelona, whose product reached the market after only a year.

It was a glorious afternoon, and I willingly agreed to

Pepe's suggestion that we go on to Pedraza. This ancient town has one of the four chief castles of Segovia, the others being at Turegono, Castilnovo and Sepulveda. An old tradition says that the Emperor Trajan was born here, although Lemprière gives the birthplace as Italica, a few miles north of Seville. Be that as it may, the town has certainly existed from Roman days and, small though it is, cut a brave figure in the history of Spain.

The drive there was memorable, with the sun on the old wrinkled hills, capped with snow and clustered with pine trees, and great ragged wounds in the earth revealing pinkish-orange stones, whose weird forms were curiously like the angels in a painting by Blake. Pedraza itself was of a rare beauty, with the old yellow castle perched on a cliff, high above the trim gardens and placidly flowing river, and still more mountains beyond. There was an old church with a magnificent font and windows, enchanting crooked streets, many of whose weathered houses bore the arms of noble or patrician families and, finest of all, a superbly proportioned Plaza Mayor, bounded by two-storied buildings, beneath, an arcade resting on mellow granite pillars, and above, balconies running all the way round. Here and there would be sudden splendid views over the countryside, and everywhere was the feel of a long, noble past. No restoration had apparently been attempted, and with luck Pedraza may escape it, for the population has dwindled and the town is all but deserted today. A little white bitch ran smilingly up, as if she had known me all her life: a tiny boy on a large horse, driving his cattle home through the town gates, solemnly lifted a hand in greeting. In the half-hour or so I spent there, these were the only living things to appear.

By now, the sun was going down, into one of the most perfect setting I ever saw. The sky was one vast sea of light and the poplars each side of the road were fiery with it, like so many fox brushes, stiff and red. Here and there were umbrella pines, black against the sky: the evening star was out already, but the voluble and persuasive Pepe talked me into going on to Turégano. The castle there was like that of

Pedraza in overlooking the town, but in a far more delapi-
dated condition: indeed, great chunks of it were rolling
about on the grass and those walls left standing seemed to
bulge a little. Yet it was imposing even in decay, particularly as to the façade which faces the town, warm rich yellow
in the dying light and surrounded by the scarred landscape
of Castille. It seemed, in fact, almost more appropriate
there in its present state than it might have been when new.
Darkness came on before I could see as much of the town as
I would have liked, and in any case, as Spanish cabbies are
wont to do, Pepe now took matters into his own hands and
set off for home, driving like a demon. Ignoring every
request to go slow, or more carefully, or even to stop altogether while I partook of a cold drink – the DYC was burning the coats of my stomach away – he swept cheerfully on,
with a muttered *Claro, claro*! or, *momentito*! or, simply *ya*!

The day, with its varied but typical occurrences, was to
be nicely rounded off with one more typical yet, indeed
quite classic. Arriving at Las Sirenas with an hour to go
before dinner, I sat down to watch the tele: a nineteenth-century drama was in progress, fantastic in its dialogue, action and mounting but nevertheless oddly familiar.
Time and again something took place that struck a chord of
recognition, until it finally dawned on me that here must be
a Spanish rendering of *The Brothers Karamasov*. As the
custom is in democratic Spain, many of the hotel staff were
watching too, and I put the question to the headwaiter, who
was standing beside my chair and complacently flicking his
coat-tails.

'Yes,' he said, 'this is the Brothers Karamason.'

'I think it is Karamasov?' I ventured to say.

'No. Karamason.'

'Truly, I have reason to believe it may be Karamasov.'

'*Karamason*,' he repeated, with emphasis and a touch of
hauteur, for Spaniards brook no contradiction.

At this point, the story having ended, the title was flashed
on to the screen, and, with a hasty 'What did I tell you?' he
was off, whisking his tails.

On a balmy day in Segovia it is quite normal to see cars with chains on the wheel and clots of snow on the body, a reminder that alpine country is not far off. Arthur Waley, the famous oriental scholar who was also a champion skier, once assured me there were no better runs than in Spain: I had put this down to a certain impishness of his, a little propensity for saying the unexpected, but now, although my own attempts to ski have always ended in ignominy, I decided to run out and see for myself.

A train brought me quickly to Cercedilla, whence the funicular to the peak of Navacerrada had just, as so often, departed, leaving time for a walk round the town. It was a typical mountain resort, all shuttered villas and closed *pensions*, with a touch of Switzerland in the older part; but here too were extensive *obras* in progress, the east wall of the parish church was wet plaster and raw-looking *viviendas* had shot up all over the hillside. Everywhere women were washing clothes and hanging them out to dry. The cafés were full of men playing cards: in winter-time, evidently, Cercedilla lives on fat accumulated in summer, when refugees pour in from the furnace of Madrid. There were marvellous views of the Siete Picos, or Seven Peaks, behind and above, and out over the immense valley; but people who live amid splendid scenery rarely look at it, Spaniards least of all.

One thing I found there of interest. Outside the public library was the usual monument to nationalists killed in the

Civil War; but the usual wording, 'fallen for God and Spain,' was amplified here to 'fallen for God, Spain and her National-syndicalist Revolution'. There was no date on this monument, either: as a rule dates are prominent. I had never seen the like of it anywhere else, and it was a rum business altogether, because the Revolution, so-called, was still undreamed of at the time and probably was the last thing the nationalists supposed they were fighting for.

A hollow whistle announced that the funicular had returned and was about to set off again. The ride up to the mountain stage was beautiful, twisting among the sunlit pine woods, with tumbling streams and sandy bridle paths among their soft green, sudden immense views of the lake caught through a clearing and the enormous boulders under a soft blue sky.

The only other travellers were a party of four, a man and three women, one of them about eighty or so and decidedly frail. What had induced her to make this trip, I could not imagine: she had to be lifted into the carriage and out again at the other end, and once she found herself on the snow, was too frightened to move. For that matter, none of us got off the platform by ourselves, the snow having been trodden until it was like a sheet of glass and no one having thought to put down cinders or gravel: we stood there, cautiously advancing a toe and pulling it back until some men in nailed boots hurried out of the bar and more or less frogmarched us to safety.

Slowly, with frequent tumbles, I made my way up the slope to the hoist. From this, small chairs slung on chains went up to the peak itself and down again, nonstop, in a circle. You had to slip deftly on to one as it passed, and then glide upward over space, as in some gigantic fun fair. The burly attendant shouted to me to fasten the belt as I set off, but I was hanging on for dear life, without a hand to spare.

It was alarming but very worth while, for the panorama from this point of vantage was magnificent, mile upon mile of other peaks all round, looking up from a lavender mist like islands in a sea, covered with dark dramatic pines, slashed with silvery streams and sparkling waterfalls. At the top another burly attendant, with a woolly bonnet and snowburnt complexion, tore me off the chair as it swung past him. I went into the bar to compose myself with a glass of anis and found a friendly talkative boy in charge there, a handsome creature with a rosy face and eyes of different colours. He insisted on treating me to another glass, and then took me to see his kitchen and *dispensa*, or pantry, as proud as any housewife, which he had every right to be: everything was spotless and it would be pleasant work preparing meals for sportsmen and mountaineers in the large orderly room with its cheerful purring stove and the breathtaking views from every window. There was hardly a skier in sight, perhaps because it was a week-day or perhaps the snow was not yet sufficiently hard; but the long even slopes, sparkling in the sun, looked inviting. When it came to getting back, however, I learned the disagreeable truth, familiar to cats, that up was one thing and down another. I simply could not bring myself to hop into the chair, which was absurd, as it moved at just the speed and height from the ground as before; but somehow to sweep downward into that huge bowl was infinitely more daunting than to swing upward to the peak. I preferred to walk down the mountainside, tobogganing down the snowfilled gullies or picking my way through the shrub and boulders. Each of these had a little collar of snow frozen hard as ice and as sharp, formed like the crystal leaves of a chandelier, tinkling underfoot. It was an exciting but comfortless walk, taking just under the hour, and I reached the bottom, bruised and cut, in the curious condition of being both bathed in sweat and with a semi-frozen behind.

A few yards from the station was the Puente Cultural, a kind of inn or rest-home for young mountaineers, apparently run or at least supported by the State. I slid down the path to it, hoping to get a meal, and found my fellow-travellers of the morning lugubriously assembled in the bar. The singular purpose of their expedition was now revealed: they had brought the old lady, their mother, to lunch up here as a treat on her eighty-fifth birthday. The Puente, however, was as far as they had managed to get and then the warden had told them they could not lunch until three. That was all the more bitter because the dining-room was full of young people eating and drinking, and bursts of their happy laughter kept coming through the door. These were the regular inmates, entitled to be fed before the stranger, but it seemed a cruel thing.

'Could we have a sandwich at least?' the man of the party asked the boy behind the bar.

'At three,' he answered, smiling. It was five past two at present.

'The funicular leaves at two-fifty.'

'So it does,' smiled the boy.

'Would they give us a sandwich in the station buffet?'

'Perhaps.'

'How, perhaps?'

'They might not have any bread.'

The birthday party took counsel together and decided to leave, coaxing the poor old woman out like a frightened horse. The boy watched them through the window, as they slithered and skated, and then turned to me.

'Does the Señora wish to eat?' he inquired politely. 'Then please go in.'

The lunch was excellent, a consommé piping hot poured from a kettle, tuna fish salad, a garlicky pork chop with artichokes, fruit and local wine, all for about fourteen shillings. Presently I heard the funicular whistle and I wondered how the luckless party had fared: life is a strange unequal business, for everyone here had eaten now and there still was plenty of food.

'Le gusta España?' asked the waitress, noting perhaps the beatific look on my face.

'Muchísimo!'

'It is a good place for foreigners,' she remarked with a sigh, echoing my own opinion exactly.

Then I dozed before a fire of blazing logs awhile, and afterwards went for another walk. There was another superb sunset that evening, the fiery rays illumining the little clouds to such a point that they were reflected in the mists below and turning the sombre pinewoods a velvety purple. At last, as night came on, I took the funicular and rattled down to Cercedilla, to sit in the station there with brownfaced men in berets playing their interminable cards amid wreaths of tobacco smoke until the Segovia train arrived.

Another expedition was to Rascafria, like Cerdecilla a bolt-hole for Madrileños in the summer, in winter loved by fishermen for the abundance of its trout. I engaged Pepe the evening before, at an agreed cost of 500 pesetas; but he must have pondered well in the night, for he now informed me the short road over the Guadarrama was shut by a snowfall and we should have to go round, which would mean 'a few kilometres more'. The few turned out to be 67, making $117\frac{1}{2}$ in all and costing 1175 pesetas. It was a mysterious trip altogether, for at one stage we were bowling merrily down the highway from France to Madrid, which we need never have touched at all. In reply to lamentations, Pepe used the simple familiar technique of producing a greasy little notebook, carefully and plainly writing 'Pts ·1175' and showing it to me in triumph, as if thereby he had clinched the matter. As he had stopped every mile or so to ask the way, I decided he was foolish rather than wicked and paid up: we shook hands and he carried my suitcase into the inn with great good humour; but a talk with the landlord later revealed that the mountain pass was open all the time.

The exterior of the Porfirio was so drab and decrepit as to be somewhat alarming: inside, it proved to be spotlessly clean and not uncomfortable, although, after basking in the tropical warmth of the Hotel Sirenas, I found it bitterly cold. When lunch-time came, I shared the experience of don Quixote on his way to Zaragoza. The menu handed to me was so extensive, it quite held the promise of his host that one here could 'pick and choose, fish or flesh, butcher's

81

meat or poultry, wild-fowl and what-not: whatever land, sea or air afford for food, it was but ask and have': but whatever I did ask for happened that day, by chance and most exceptionally, to be 'off'. In the end I followed Sancho's example and prayed them to bring what they had: don Quixote got a dish of cowheel with onions, I a rabbit stew, but apart from that the cases seemed identical.

The dining-room also had to serve as lounge, bar and television parlour. The only other people there were a woman and her teenage daughter, knitting while they watched the tele and waited for their husband and father. He had gone fishing first thing in the morning and now, at two o'clock, there was still no sign of him. He would be in presently, the fishing-widow remarked with a sigh, gulp down a little food and be off at once 'until the setting of the sun'. This happened every day he got off from his work in Madrid. Bravely the pair of them sat and knitted until at three o'clock the mother suddenly threw her needles aside and exclaimed: 'Enough! We will eat!'

'If we can eat without him at three, why not at half past two?' the daughter asked, in a distinctly peevish tone, but with a certain logic, to which Mamma made no reply.

After the meal, I went on foot to the Cartuja de el Paular, an ancient monastery listed by Turismo as keeping a guest-house for travellers. The few people I met on the road all gave me a pleasant greeting, but they had a mournful air about them and every single woman was dressed in black. A boiling stream ran alongside much of the way, with fisher-men at every fifty yards or so; but the fish would scarcely bother to take their bait in such turbulent water, and indeed the baskets all were empty. No cars were to be seen, only great black oxen with sweeping horns that slowly drew waggons piled with timber; and altogether the prospect, with snow falling thick, was one of desolation.

The old Carthusian abbey dates from 1390: in 1836 the monks were expelled by decree, like all the religious orders: in 1876, the building was declared a national monument: and in 1954 it was handed over to the Benedictines. I was visiting it both for the sake of its church and with an idea of moving into the guest-house, for nothing Benedictines do is ever done badly and I could see that the charms of my inn would presently be exhausted.

On reaching it, however, I found developments of an all too familiar kind. The fathers were pent up in one corner and the greater part was made into a *parador*, one of the worst I had seen. More and more, the simplicity and sober good taste of these hotels when they originally started is giving way to a stereo-typed chichi; and here, as well as the enormous artificial candles and *típico* furnishing, there were bad contemporary pictures of monks in every room. A misguided attempt had been made to preserve the devotional atmosphere that is so pleasant a thing in houses run by monks; and for me the whole thing was best summed up by the principal courtyard, restored to the point of lifelessness and labelled *Patio del Ave Maria*.

The church, gravely damaged in the earthquake of 1755, was also much restored; but it had a splendid grille by Juan Frances and a superb Gothic altar-piece in glowing alabaster, said to be Genoese. There was no heating of any kind, and the very stones and flags seemed to give off an icy cold. Chilled to the core of my being, I soon retired to the overheated *parador* in search of reviving coffee. But all the waiters were clustered round the tele, deep in a bullfight, and my efforts to attract their attention came to nothing. There must be a way of diverting Spaniards from a spectacle that absorbs them, but I have never found it out.

It was snowing even harder on the homeward journey, and by the time I got in I had a feverish cold that kept me in bed for a couple of days. I lay under a pile of blankets, wearing my warmest clothes, with a woolly hat on my head, but even so there was no getting warm. The hardy folk who ran the place had never heard of hot-water bottles, but they kindly put some tepid water in a lemonade bottle and brought me that. After this, they never once came to ask how I was or if there was anything else I wanted. This was not due to hardness of heart, for they were good friendly people: it was simply, I believe, that the eye is all in Spain and when Spaniards do not actually see you they are prone to forget your existence.

It was a Sunday evening when I reappeared and the place was full of weekend fishermen from Madrid, talking only of fish. There were also numbers of dogs: it is the fashion these days to have a dog, or preferably more than one, the larger the better, and to take them everywhere, even into the dining-room. Furthermore, they are allowed to behave as badly there as if they were Spanish children: they bark fiercely at each other and put their paws on the table, without discomposing their masters in the least.

I sat by the fire and read *Ama*, a weekly for suburban housewives. This was not done of choice, but because I had brought no books with me and *Ama* was the only printed matter in the house. There was not so much as a newspaper and in fact no newspapers were to be had in the *pueblo*, Carmen the innkeeper's daughter said, because nobody ever read one. And so I read *Ama* from cover to cover, and grisly enough it was. I recall one advertisement of an 'original way to serve drinks' – you put the drink in a miniature copy of the Mannekenpiss (Little Pissing Man) at Brussels, pressed a button, and the drink squirted from the appropriate organ into the glass, causing general mirth and *alegría* at party or fiesta.

No doubt in honour of the full house, quite a few items on the menu were available that evening. A friend in Madrid had told me that Rascafria was famous for *jamon serrano*, or raw cured ham, and it was listed here as Especial de la Casa. When it came, it was so tough that, chew as I might, I could make no impression on it. Rather than upset Carmen by leaving it on the plate, I threw it all on the blazing logs, and twenty minutes afterwards it was still smouldering and perfectly recognizable. But there was freshly caught trout as well, and good local wine, delicious oranges and excellent coffee: if the food was poor on the whole, it was probably due to lack of custom.

A lorry driver came in and sat at the table next to mine.

He had the real Castilian face, long, bony and ironic, which marked him out from the plump and pallid specimens of Spain's emerging middle-class, whose sporting pretensions he lost no time in deriding.

'Such childishness!' he said, looking them over with contempt. 'How can they waste their time upon it?' He spoke freely, as working men often do to foreigners, and proved to be an unsparing critic of everything that cropped up, the Government, the weather, the traffic in Madrid, the clergy and, above all, Spain herself. A dapper little man with a smooth señorito's face appeared on the tele and gave a talk on the Life and Work of a Policeman. 'All nonsense,' my new acquaintance growled, after a few minutes. 'Tonterías! it is not like that at all.' And he proceeded to give me the truth about police activities, which consisted mainly of hurrying, abusing and fining decent lorry drivers like himself or standing about in bars. I spent a most enjoyable hour in his company, and when I left he rose and bowed with all the old traditional courtesy of his kind, now vanishing fast.

In the small hours of the morning tumult broke out as the fishermen prepared to drive back to their offices in Madrid. No one troubled to lower his voice in the sleeping house, and the dogs all barked vivaciously at the thought of a ride in the car. I listened awhile in mounting fury, then decided to get up as well and take the coach to Madrid, en route for Segovia: it was an immense detour, but the alternative was another ruinous trip by taxi. Rain was pouring down, and the prospect of a second day by the fire, without even a second issue of *Ama*, held little attraction.

Rascafria must be one of those numerous *pueblos* where the women do all the work. Already at half past six they were up and about, driving goats or cows or dragging heavy bundles of firewood, passing each other with a mournful *adiós!* and nothing more. There was not a man to be seen, except for the other travellers, who trickled down the road one by one, all in a state of hilarity which I ascribed to the fact that they were about to leave their natal town. The coach stood waiting by the bridge, but the doors were locked, and the ticket office too was shut and in darkness. But as we stood and shivered, the sordid café by the bridge, where an idiot always mopped and mowed, threw open its doors: the men all rushed inside and ordered *copitas*, and were rounded up with difficulty when at last the driver and the conductor appeared. They were a festive bunch, to be sure: in every village we came to, a great many, for the bus meandered about the country collecting all with business in Madrid, the jolly fellows leaped out to resume their drinking and had to be hunted up again. On the journey they laughed and sang and made jokes that grew broader and broader, until the conductor sternly bade them hold their peace.

Once we had left the muddy country lanes and taken the smooth high road to the capital, the land on either side was dotted with new chalets and villas, horrid messes of wrought iron, fancy paintwork or stippling, with little gardens crying out for the plaster gnomes, rabbits and toadstools offered now for sale on the once austere Recoletos in Madrid. It was an extraordinary thing to see. There was the country all spread out, grim and magnificent with its huge boulders, rocky canyons, torrential streams and dark sinister ilex, with the Sierras lowering on the horizon; and in the foreground everywhere, the awful little status symbols of the new Spain.

And, apparently, worse things still were afoot. The man next to me said with pride that Madrid and Segovia had agreed on a plan to develop the whole Sierra: among much else, they meant to build 30,000 flats in Rascafria itself. Various bodies interested in nature and wild life were opposing them but, said the man, they were *entremetidos*, busybodies, and would surely fail.

It is a dismal thought, but Spain seems determined to develop herself to death. All through the day the memory of that polluted landscape kept recurring and recurring, and it was a huge relief to arrive in Segovia once more, knowing that, like Venice, she cannot be spoiled.

9

My last morning in Segovia came, and I went for a final
stroll through her lovely streets before catching a train for
Avila. Due perhaps to the approach of Christmas, the city
was rife with baby pigs, kicking and crying in sacks, ranged
in macabre rows on the butchers' slab or, roasted brown,
staring appalled from a dish in a tavern window, grimly
parodying the Massacre of the Innocents. It being a
Thursday, there was an open air market near the Plaza de
Dr Alguna, a sophisticated one too, for as well as the usual
heaps of fruit, vegetables, eggs, loaves and cheeses there
was a bookstall with a glorious collection of trash, comics,
falangist propaganda and magazines devoted to love, with
names like *Romeo y Julieta* or *Cúpido*. Various bookworms
were browsing here but did not buy, in spite of the owner
bellowing that all prices were greatly reduced and a chance
like this would never come again. There were displays of
clothing, mini-skirts and slacks, weird and marvellous
underwear, and articles for the household, terrible antima-
cassars, embroidered chairbacks and plush tablecloths
fringed with bobbles for a great occasion. People picked up
anything that took their fancy, cake, sausage or cheese, to
prod and smell, while dogs roamed freely about, sniffing
and squirting the vegetables on the ground. Everyone
seemed to enjoy the fun immensely, and so did I.

Presently I returned to the hotel to collect my luggage
and bid farewell to Botones who, regarding my account as

closed, watched me leave with frank indifference. Pepe drove me to the station, in a fit of sulks, for he had proposed coming all the way to Avila itself. He had never been there, he said, and it was a place that every man should visit once: money was no object with the Señora and the trains were terrible. He was correct in the latter statement. Between Segovia and Villalba, the particularly choice specimen I took paused an hour at Collado Mediano, a tiny place where it should never have stopped at all. Friends in Madrid had asserted such things no longer happened and, strangely, I had believed them. Spurred on by famine – it was ten past three – I jumped down and made for the buffet, followed by shouts from the driver and guard that the train was about to start. There was ample time, however, for a *bocadillo*, or Little Mouthful, a curious term for a long roll of hard bread split open and filled with slices of *chorizo* tough as leather. To help matters on I asked for a tumbler of wine, which the barlady poured with reluctance, plainly thinking the request a wild one, and which was so liberally watered, it would scarce have affected a baby. At Villalba there was another hour to wait and little to see, the town having become a dreary mess of haphazard jerry-building, streets of no character, supermarkets and garages: it could have been anywhere in Europe, were it not for the thin grubby dogs doing their round of the garbage pails and, on this freezing day, the women washing clothes in the river, kneeling on the bank, rubbing and rinsing, just as in the torrid evenings of summer.

Darkness was coming on when at length, after many a meditative pause, our train limped into Avila station. The difference between this austere little town and gay Segovia made itself felt at once, for there the streets would be filling up with people bent on enjoying themselves, and here they were all but deserted, with only a few muffled figures hurrying homeward to warmth under the sparse dim lights that burned on the walls.

Next morning, however, all was bustle and animation. The sound of voices grew steadily as one approached the *plaza* until, in the market itself, it swelled to the rumbling roar that only Spanish throats can produce. Friday was market day here, and it was a real earthy market with none of Segovia's frills and fripperies. The middle of the square was given up to mounds of red and white cabbage, the size of footballs, huge onions with glossy skins, red chilli peppers, branches of bay tree, different types of salad and one enormous orange marrow that would have needed an axe, if not a circular saw, to cut it. On the street kerbs there were various specialities. One corner was entirely given up to garlic, enough to flavour the whole province, the heads attached to plaited green rush in a decorative way; and very beautiful the garlic was, pure silver or tinted with purple or rose, with the luminous quality of its skin and the delicate fluting of the cloves. Another corner had nothing but eggs, deep brown instead of the usual dead white, and live fowls, indignant or alarmed, held head downward or crammed into boxes. An old man in a black corduroy suit and a beret was pacing up and down with three newly slain kids over his shoulder. The walls were festooned with shiny yellow *tripas*, far from appetizing but essential as cases for sausages and *morcillos*, the spicy black puddings typical of the region. One kiosk had saddles, with raised wooden sides front and back and covered with sheepskin, of a pattern that went back over the centuries, and there were stirrups, boots, walking sticks, paniers, bells for goats and cows, all homely and rustic in appearance. A man sat on the kerb and split logs into kindling, for starting up the primitive charcoal braziers on which the women of the countryside still do their cooking.

The clamour was mostly conversation, for while there were cries of 'Good chickens here' or 'My garlic is cheap' from the women, there was little huckstering. Mules laden with more wares poured continually into the *plaza*, to the confusion of any motorist unwise enough to enter it. A mighty hold-up, amounting to general paralysis of the traffic, was caused by a single diminutive ass, who had taken his stand in the middle of the road and resolutely declined to budge. And presently women who had spent hours in research and argument over the prices could be seen going home with half a loaf, a couple of eggs, a lemon or two or a cauliflower. By late afternoon the whole square was empty again, but for the municipal workmen sweeping up the refuse.

I spent the day revisiting old familiar places, remembered in blazing sunlight, yet somehow more truly themselves under a lowering winter sky. The Cathedral looked particularly at home in bleak surroundings, a grand severe building designed as a fortress too and serving as such from the eleventh to the sixteenth century, until the squabbles that arose from its dual function became a *molestia*. Here in 1158 the sturdy townsfolk proclaimed Alonzo VIII, a child of four, their rightful king, as he was, and defended him against a wicked uncle for seven years until the danger was past: here again, sturdy as ever, in 1465 they enthroned an effigy of Enrique IV, whom they did not care for, then tore off his royal appurtenances, sceptre, crown and robes, kicked the denuded figure over and proclaimed his brother Alonzo instead.

Inside, all was darker still, but a dim light from an upper window fell on the grandiose alabaster tomb of Alfonso Tostado. He was bishop here in 1449 and is Avila's leading, if not, to be sure, her only intellectual. He is shown in episcopal fig, mitre and all, composing for dear life, with a look about his eyes as if he had done so a long long time by very poor light. Not a day went by but he covered three pages at least, with wholesome accurate Catholic doctrine that opened the eyes of the blind. That is what the memorial inscription tells us; but Ford, on the other hand, calls him a *burro cargado de letras* and says unkindly that his 60,255 sheets of 'unmitigated prose, and dissertations on broomsticks, are now fortunately food, or rather poison, for worms'. It is no small marvel that Ford ever left Spain in one piece.

Whether because of the cold or because it was market day, there was not a soul about, rare in this country where people, men and women alike, still drop into places of worship for a quick prayer or a word with a favourite saint. An air of neglect, that I did not remember, hung over the chapels, with their dusty paper flowers and grubby lace. In that of St Nicola was a collecting box for the dowries of orphan girls, a pretty thought, but the coin I dropped in met with no answering chink. I tried turning on various switches here and there, but no light came.

I went on to the convent of San José, the first that Teresa of Avila ever founded, on St Bartholomew's day, 1562, the church being completed only after her death. The shadowy figure of Mary's husband played a tremendous part in Teresa's spiritual life: over and over again we come on references to 'this most glorious saint', 'this blessed saint', 'this glorious patriarch' in her writings. She tells us that, having been in authority over our Lord on earth, he has only to ask in heaven for his wish to be granted. 'I know not how any man can think of the Queen of the angels, during the time that she suffered so much with the infant Jesus, without giving thanks to St Joseph for the services he rendered them then', she remarks in her autobiography. It is interesting, because in the popular Catholic tradition of Spain, St Joseph was anything but an agreeable character. There is a legend of Mary, tired, hot and thirsty, asking him to pick some cherries for her, and of his sour reply, 'Let him that got thee with child pick thy cherries', whereupon the tree bowed over until she could reach them. In our day, the dry sherry Tio Pepe is laughingly named for him, 'Uncle Joe', *tio* meaning however not only uncle but also a sharp-tongued awkward person. But Teresa assures us, from her own experience, that he can obtain more blessings and favours than any other saint in heaven. He stands on the altar of her church, not the venerable man we are accustomed to see, but young, handsome and dashing, something perhaps like an officer in the Great Armada, carrying the child in his arms, each wearing a golden crown.

This convent, which is also known as that of The Mothers, was founded in 1562, when the saint was forty-seven. There was a fierce opposition to it on the part of the town council, which she reports but does not explain, and which may well have had its root in simple male chauvinism. As the council intended to thwart her by refusing the site, she persuaded her brother-in-law to acquire a house privily, putting it in his wife's name, for this saint never baulked at diddling the devil when need arose. It was a small tumbledown building then, but she personally set about its repair with her usual determination, performing a miracle en passant, as it were, when her nephew was killed by falling masonry and she brought him back to life. Later of course it was embellished with paintings and carving, particularly fine being that on the choirstalls where, it is said, the nuns would never sit, believing them to have been occupied by angels whenever the saint heard mass; and there are ornate tombs, some of them splendid, of various companions and relations.

What the nuns prize most, however, are the relics of the saint herself. They have the drum she played at Christmas, the stairway down which the devil threw her, a belt and handkerchief, the jug she drank from, the nut-tree she planted, a letter she wrote and, best of all, her clavicula, a brown dusty bone set in silver with emeralds and pearls. The sister who displayed it hovered about in a kind of rapture, for all the countless times she must have seen it before. The importance of bones to the religious in Latin countries is difficult perhaps for others to grasp; but there is and always has been no end of jealous heartburning about their often disputed possession. Never shall I forget the complacency of a nun at the sister Carmelite foundation here, as she showed me the saint's ring-finger and two bones of St John of the Cross with the remark, 'More than they have at San José.'

Whether it was the absence of pilgrims today, or merely a chance mood of my own, for the first time San José seemed more of a show-place than a centre of life. Rather than risk finding the same at other points of the via Teresiana, I walked to the Monasterio Real de Santo Tomás beyond the city wall. Not so long ago it stood among wide bare fields, but the urbanizing demon has crept towards it and now knocks at its very gate. In summer there is wont to be a horde of Yanqui tourists milling around in the church, chattering and wise-cracking at the top of their lungs: at present it was deserted except for a Dominican father dozing in one of the confessionals and a workman engaged, with many a splutter and crackle, in adjusting a microphone.

It is a Gothic building, noble inside and out, its greatest treasures being an altarpiece by Berruguete and carven choirstalls reputed to be the finest in Spain. These however are in a gallery on high, within the *clausura*, and may only be viewed by men. I had been rather hoping that the fresh winds, if not gales, that blow from the Vatican these days might have swept this medieval absurdity away, but it was still in force and will doubtless continue to the end of time. In the church, too, is the most elaborate monument in all Avila, the tomb of don Juan, only son of the Catholic Kings, who was killed by ruffians at Salamanca in 1497, aged nineteen. The death of this valiant and gifted boy was a catastrophe for the nation, raised up in glory by Ferdinand and Isabel only to pass under Charles V, whose heart and mind were fixed elsewhere. Some have attributed this exquisite memorial to Domenico of Florence, others to Fancelli, but in either case it bears comparison with the royal tombs of Granada.

I was feasting my eyes upon it when a loudspeaker near at hand broke into a confused and amazing mutter. Looking round for the cause, I perceived that with typical insouciance the workmen had left the microphone switched on and leaning against the confessional, and that a penitent was now innocently broadcasting his deeds to the world at large. Fantastic, farcical things come about in this land through sheer inattention to detail. The brusque asides, during mass, of clergy who forget their microphone, I regard as lawful entertainment; but this was another kettle of fish and I scrupulously took to my heels.

Everyone, male or female, is allowed to walk in the cloisters, with their splendid arches and vaulted ceilings. The sky had turned clear and blue, and the sun was shining on the courtyard gardens, where a rosebush or two was still in flower. Evidently some of the rooms were still used for classes and lectures: through a heavy door with *Ethica et Metaphysica Specialis* inscribed on it in faded Gothic letters, came a nasal voice which uttered arresting statements about the relation of soul to body at dictation speed. In the Cloister of Silence, there was a tiny confessional set in the wall with a quotation from St Teresa marked beside it, of how she saw our Lady put a cope of exceeding whiteness on the Dominican father, Pedro Ibañez her confessor, who supported her in the battle of San José. The little wooden doors were unlocked, and the box inside with its minute stone bench looked as if meant for a child or a doll. And there was the sacristy with everything shipshape, the mass towels spotless, the vestments all neatly folded up and put away in labelled drawers, the floor swept, the tables polished, with a more than housewifely care.

For all the medieval atmosphere, there was nothing of a museum about Santo Tomás. At the porter's lodge there was a busy coming and going of people, lay and religious. Two little boys trotted in, wanting greenery for their Christmas decorations – the Yuletide customs of the north have taken hold of Spain in recent years – and the porter smilingly fetched them boughs of fir from a cache. More boys followed and were briskly turned away, the porter recollecting that he had supplied them a week ago. Monks from other Dominican houses, travelling light, were looking for bed and board, and he waved them on into the enclosure. An old peasant woman brought a letter, for someone learned to read and explain. A mother discussed her baby's christening, as anxiously as if no baby had ever been christened before. And the porter ran to and fro on his errands, dashed up to newcomers, saw others out, like a friendly watchful sheepdog.

In the afternoon I walked out to the Sanctuary of Sonsoles, five kilometres away and, built on a prominence,
the ideal spot for a view of Avila. It was painful to see how
urbanización was blurring the stark tremendous lines of the
city. The Sanctuary itself was charming as always, with its
simple church, stone benches and tables under the trees
outside, the weather-beaten fountain and roomy old barns,
all set in an expanse of soft green grass. In summer the
place is thronged by pilgrims, who bring baskets of food
and, once they have paid their respects to the Virgin, make
merry the livelong day to the blithe howl of transistors.
Even now the church was a-glimmer with little lights, not
candles but primitive oil rushes, such as formerly lit the
streets of Vatican City on great church occasions. La
Santísima Virgen de Sonsoles was smartly dressed and, surrounded by angels, hugged her Son, a doll with a curiously
middle-aged face, to her bosom with a rather priggish air.
Plaques revealed that she had been crowned protectress of
Avila in the Cathedral there, by the Bishop, on August 15,
1934; and a good day's work it was, for she later prevented
the marxist hordes from seizing the town. To mark its
appreciation, she was conducted hither in the triumphant
year of 1939, to serve as a pattern of faith and devotion for
generations to come.

The official booklet on Avila, by the well known novelist
Camillo José Cela, makes no reference at all to Sonsoles,
and even the fullest guides give it a bare mention; but
Spain is so rich in delectable places like this, there cannot
be room to speak of them all. Walking home was better still
than coming, for with time to spare I could leave the road,
treading fields of thyme that smelled deliciously underfoot,
wandering down the banks of a river, passing little *cortijas*
with their rich familiar scent of pig, exchanging a word
with countrymen as they rode their buxom waterpots to
the well or directed their flocks and herds towards home.
The air was full of the sound of bells, soft and plaintive,
and the few little clouds in the sky were turning rosy as the
sun went down. About a mile from the city wall I stopped

at a wayside inn and was served by a woman of such melancholy mien, she looked like despair in person. She appeared to act as a butt for the local wits, which may have had something to do with the matter. A group of men were teasing her as I went in, alleging that her drinks were mostly water and contaminated water at that, and when she charged me a penny for a big glass of wine, they all shouted together that it was outrageous and I was not to dream of paying.

'Let her chalk it up,' bawled one. 'You can settle another year.' And, overcome by his brilliance, the horrid bunch went into fits of laughter.

Dusk had fallen when I reached Avila. In every café the television was bellowing full tilt, the customers, their lined faces blue in the glare of the screen, listening enthralled with open mouths. In my hotel there was an innovation I had not grasped the night before, in the shape of a 'Club', a bar furnished in gaudy avant-garde style and full of boys and girls, smartly dressed, fondling each other as if no one else were present. They seemed an anomaly in the decorous old Reina Isabel, and still more so in the birth-place of St Teresa: indeed, the sense I got of a culture swiftly, dizzily, transformed was overpowering. Only when I went to dinner, and the elderly waiter brought the classic meal, the cool vegetable soup, weary *merluza*, chicken of experience and 'flan', could I feel that all continuity was not yet lost.

10

Avila was warming up for Christmas. From six in the morning till noon her church bells lifted their tinny admonishing
voices. The old women in black who toddle to Mass every
day of the year were now accompanied by daughters,
granddaughters and babies in arms, while a sprinkling of
men tagged along in the rear. As the afternoon wore on,
another, bacchanalian, mood took over and the city became
a jungle. Bands of youths roamed the streets, creating
uproar with tambourines, guitars and *zambombas*. The last
are a rustic instrument, hide being stretched over the
mouth of a jar and rubbed with the palm of the hand,
producing an eerie, faintly sinister, whine, similar to that
of Orange drums in the north of Ireland. The youths also
shouted and sang and refreshed themselves from bottles:
as always at times of popular rejoicing, the ground was
littered with broken glass.

Fights were plentiful, some half-hearted, others in
earnest. On Christmas Eve in the Plaza de Sta Teresa
two men drew knives on each other, observed but not
reproved by the policeman on point duty. 'I am here to
control the traffic,' he seemed to say. 'A jaywalker I
would denounce, a misparked car need expect no mercy,
but the mere slitting of throats is no concern of mine.'
Nor, had he wished to intervene, could he easily have
done it, for he stood pent up in a wall, waist-high, of
hams, cheeses, fruits, skins of wine and bottles of liqueur,

which the citizens of Spain offer their police at the Nativity.

This pleasant custom had let me in for a few bad moments earlier in the day, when a couple of *guardias* stopped me in the *plaza* and gravely inquired my name and place of residence in town. My passport was valid, my conscience clear, yet this sudden inquiry out of the blue filled me with dread. The *guardias* impassively noted the particulars, said I should hear from them and continued unsmiling on their way, leaving me to my troubled thoughts. But the man who roasted chestnuts on the corner was able to reassure me.

'Don't worry,' he said. 'You left a bottle of anis for the cops this morning, didn't you? They are going to send you a Christmas card.'

In due course it was delivered to my hotel, a Disneyish Mother and Child, with some flowery words of good will.

I had been at some pains to inquire about midnight Masses, hoping to hear somewhere the Escolanía San Pedro. It is the second best choir in the land for liturgy and for carols (*villancicos*), the first being the choir of Monserrat, and is said to perform at Christmas. At the Cathedral a sacristan asserted that it would definitely sing that night at the *Misa cantada del gallo*, and I turned up full of the most lively anticipation. Why I persist in believing what such people tell me, is hard to say: it may well be a case of what Mother Church categorizes as 'incorrigible stupidity' and treats with compassion. There was a sung Mass all right, sparsely attended and held in one of the chapels, but no sign of any choir. The organ moaned and wheezed and a few canons, tucked away behind the altar, wheezed in company, either a few bars ahead or a few behind, or singing a different tune altogether. Every twenty seconds or so the door shrieked like a terrified pig as the latecomers walked in. If I were asked to name the most characteristic Spanish sound, I would vote for the screech of unoiled hinges in cathedral doors: I would indeed, in preference even to the rasping hoick! of a man preparing to spit. When Mass was over, we filed up to the altar and with the utmost solemnity kissed the dimpled celluloid knee of the Child. Spain is apparently getting some fussy American notions, for the sacristan, the same worthless wretch who had misled me about the choir, stood by with a cloth, wiping the knee after every kiss. A tray was placed beside the crib for offerings, but no one responded.

The Cathedral was cold and draughty and, once the organ and the canons had finished wheezing, glumly silent. It was odd to go out into the crowded streets and hear the shindy raging as before. It continued without remorse into the early hours, swelled by an influx of students in their festive *traje*, white neck-ruff, black velvet doublet, knee breeches and cloak, with long gaily coloured ribbons streaming from the collar, who tangled violently with the local boys in the traditional way of town and gown.

The name given these student bands is *tuna*, which in the exact sense means a truant-playing or wild loose way of life. When I got to my hotel, a *tuna* stood by the door, lustily singing that well-known ditty *El Relicario;* but just then a head poked out of a window and bade them enter, whereupon they broke off at once and hurried inside. Having made a tour of the guests, shaking a tambourine under their noses for contributions, they settled down to enjoy the cakes and wine the landlord offered, laughing and talking, singing if asked and turning somersaults whether asked or not, with unflagging brio, in spite of the numerous calls they had already paid that evening. They were not real university men but pupils of the local *Instituto General*, and one of them confided to me how much he would like to be at Granada, where his cousin was. He spoke so wistfully, I thought he was thirsting for an education beyond the resources of Avila to supply; but it transpired in the course of discussion that what chiefly appealed to him was the proximity of Málaga airport.

'The last time my cousin was there with the *tuna*,' said the aspiring scholar, with kindled eye, 'they took over two thousand pesetas. Foreigners going away and pesetas no

Universitas
BIBLIOTHECA
Otaviensis

good any more, they empty their pockets just like that. And all running about and losing their luggage . . . my cousin says, they don't even expect you to sing.'

It was after four when I got to bed, and there was no sleeping then. Avila held carouse: I lay listening to it, and to the shrieks of passing trains, answered by other shrieks from afar. In the normal Spanish run, there is a brief hiatus between the last sounds of night and those that herald the day. On this occasion they overlapped, so that shouts and drumming and the crash of glass vied with clamour of bells and the shindy of garbage collectors. The citizens, other than those involved, slept happily through it all. At ten o'clock no one answered my urgent rings for coffee, nor was there a sign of life downstairs except for the night watchman, supine on the parlour Chesterfield and snoring his head off; and the streets of the town were all but deserted.

After roaming a while I came on a small workman's café that was open and in the care of a heavy-eyed boy of seven or eight. Yawning, he said the family was asleep and he could not work the coffee machine, nor was there any bread. Today was *fiesta*, he pointed out, and the café would have been shut but for pity of those who must work as usual, namely the dustmen. They had broken their fast on brandy or anis and sugary cakes, to which I was welcome. Declining the cake, I begged for some brandy. Taking a bottle of Fundador from the shelf in both little hands, he started pouring it into a *cana*, with the clear intention of filling this up to the brim. I suggested it was rather a lot and he replied, looking hurt, that no one else had complained.

To instruct a Spaniard of any age whatever is foolish, indeed impossible; but the row of empty bottles on the shelf, with their promise of trouble in store, impelled me to have a try.

'There is no complaint,' I said. 'Only, some drinks cost more than others. The cana you have there is for wine, which is cheap. Those small glasses are for brandy, because it is dear.'

The little chap looked at me in a daze. 'How do you

mean, dear?' he demanded. 'It is written up there on the board, what it costs. You can see for yourself and give me the money. That is what everyone does.' And he pushed the brimming beaker crossly over the bar.

By now the pedagogue in me was fully awake.

'If you serve the brandy in *canas*,' I hammered on, 'you will get less for a bottleful than you had to pay for the bottle itself. You will be losing money, not making it. Which is *disparates*.'

'You had better wait till my father comes,' said the boy. 'He will explain things to you.'

I had no intention at all of being there when papa arrived to see how trade had flourished in his absence. Accepting defeat, I paid and went, leaving the brandy untouched for very shame and the perplexed little boy staring after me.

At Santo Tomás there was a Mass beautifully sung and conducted, so far removed from the performance at the Cathedral as to seem like something else altogether. There was a charming crib as well, with virile Castilian shepherds guarding camels half their size and sheep that were bigger than cradle, Child and Mary in one, while a handsome if unexpected Roman palace was wreathed in branches of pine and spruce from the woods around. Fathers lifted their babies to see it, old peasants knelt in adoration, a chubby colonel in full dress with sash and sword finished a prayer by blowing a kiss, women lit candle after candle to swell the shimmering blaze from a votive stand near by, while the organ softly played *Adeste Fideles* with never a wrong note.

From there I walked out along the river and up the rocky slopes to the Cuatro Postes, the simple cross in a square of Grecian columns which marks the spot where little Teresa de Jesús and her brother, running away in search of martyrdom, were caught and taken home by a worldly uncle. No one was about today and not a sound to be heard but the bells of sheep grazing alone and the trill of a lark, duped perhaps by the sun into believing that spring was at hand. The sky was mirrored in the waters of the Adaja, threading the yellows and silvery greys of cliff and boulder with a ribbon of blue. Avila, mercifully out of earshot, looked her noble self again.

I sat on a rock and basked in the warmth like a lizard until the pangs of hunger drove me back to the town. In the hotel they had pinned up a menu for the gala luncheon today. It was written in a flowing hand and rife with arabesques, a work of art whose form, however, surpassed its content. There was to be vegetable soup, *merluza* and chicken, but in place of the 'flan' was the national sweetmeat, *turrón*. This varies from region to region, but the basic ingredients are constant, nuts and sugar, or honey, and it is amazing what can be wrought with such simple harmless stuff. Now it emerges as a cracktooth bake; anon, it blends in a nougat, glueing the jaws together like putty; or it assumes the air of a soft and creamy fudge, deceitfully, as it turns to dust in the mouth and settles until washed down. One form or another is as sure to appear on Christmas tables in Spain as plum pudding and mince pies are in England.

I went on to Old Pepillo, a restaurant where food and wine were always excellent and where the bourgeoisie was wont to celebrate weddings and christenings in sober decorous fashion. It was quite transformed, the jungle life of the streets having surged in even there. People were shouting and babies yelling, bottles were overturning, drunks falling off their chairs, newcomers bawling for service, the rest gobbling as if they had never seen food before. Flurried waiters, crimson and panting, struggled through the seething mass holding the trays above their heads to be out of harm's way. The *mayor domo* brusquely motioned me to a table where someone already sat, a thing that had never happened to me in Spain before. I asked the incumbent if I were molesting: he looked up from the Pekinese in his lap, whom he was plying with anis, and with a vague dissociated grin assured me I was not.

All in all, the atmosphere today was nordic. From a table near to ours there came, at intervals evenly spaced, a reverberating belch. The only items missing in fact, were the paper hats, an omission that time will doubtless make good. To cut things short, I asked for an omelette and salad and nothing else. The waiter echoed the words with a bitter ringing laugh and dashed away.

My stable companion was laughing too. 'Today is Christmas,' he revealed. 'Omelette, salad. . .' He sizzled over another word for a while, then gave it up. 'Omelette, salad, nada,' he said. 'Are you fond of dogs? I am very fond of dogs. This fellow drinks like a man.' And he offered his glass again to the Pekinese, who with moist and goggling eyes lapped away with a will.

The waiter banged down a dish and darted off, without removing the cover.

'Suspended!' my companion succeeded in bringing out, with an air of triumph. 'The lista. Christmas. Same for everyone today.'

Slowly, with a premonition of evil, I raised the cover. There lay half a tiny pig, the ear roasted to a biscuit, the little trotters drawn up, the brain oozing over the snout, a little blue eye half open. Hastily I clapped the cover down and leaned back in my chair. Then more bangs announced the delivery of a jug of fine rich Cebreros and a beautifully baked roll, the crust adorned with leaves and flowers as if intended for exhibition; and of this I made my Christmas dinner, thinking I could do, and often had done, very much worse.

Travellers are a possessive lot. They somehow feel that a place they love should remain for ever fixed in a mould, so that with every visit they can take up precisely where they left off before. Changes, even for the better, afflict them with a sense of personal loss. Well I knew that not so long ago the plebeian crowd in Pepillo's, enjoying itself with such gusto, could never have crossed its threshold. Some would have been glad enough to collect a few scraps from the kitchen door. Good things then were for other people, shops and cafés and restaurants, places to walk straight past, so far beyond reach that one scarcely looked in the window. To resent the new way of life would have been wrong, and I did not; in fact I rejoiced at it, or at least at its implication. But the noise, the tippling, the brawls in the public places, the vulgarity – here, in Teresa's birthplace, where vulgarity was once unknown – were too much for me. On a sudden impulse I ran back to the hotel, asked for the bill and caught the evening coach to Madrigal de Las Altas Torres.

Simply to be moving away brings relief at such times, but I was not yet out of the wood. The coach was packed with country folk, a high proportion of whom had also been at the bottle. I think I never saw so many drunks at a time before, not even at a fair in the west of Ireland. Among the party were a group of gipsies, two of them youths, attired in pink pleated shirts of which they were strangely proud. One of these harangued the assembly in a hoarse voice the whole journey long, a matter of two and a half hours, until I could have cheerfully throttled him. There was also a dumb man of the kind so often met in Spain, who felt impelled to take the centre of the stage and direct the affairs of everyone else. His conversation consisted of a monotonous kkkhhh kkkhhh kkkhhh, his thought being otherwise conveyed in pantomime, as he helped people on and off whether they liked it or not, waved his arms at the drunken gipsy, whose competition he appeared to resent, and sparred with the conductor. That person, in black beret and blue overalls, was a mixture of genius and saint, imperturbably collecting fares from bodies packed like sardines, smiling tenderly at the inebriated, hastening to the succour of those that were sick, remembering at every stop what luggage the departing ones had brought and winkling it out of the wild confusion on the roof.

As we had left at five o'clock, it was soon too dark to see a great deal of the country. I remember a stretch of mile upon mile of pine woods, with sandy soil and bridle paths running through, and was just thinking how much like parts of Surrey it was when suddenly there rode out a whole posse of swarthy peasants on mules, with blankets over their heads like Red Indians. Then on we went through the gathering night, in the jolting airless bus, the noise getting worse all the time, until I thought my head would split. But all bad things come to an end and presently the conductor shouted 'Madrigal!' with an air of exultation, as if he had not been sure of our making it. I went straight to the Posada de Madrigal, yet another *parador*, newly done up, with gleaming bath and fittings, garish paintings on the walls, a wealth of wrought-iron fantasies, polished floors, folksy rugs, everything in true suburban taste, down to the gimmicky bar and the Alsatian puppy. It was a proof of my lowered condition that it all seemed perfectly splendid.

11

Madrigal de las Altas Torres lies in one of the vast steppes so typical of this region. There is no hill or even rise from which the town can be viewed as a whole. In its day it was ringed by a massive wall which formed a perfect circle, unique of its kind in the country, and people could only pass in and out through four immense gateways. Today but three are left, of which one is slowly tumbling down, while the gaps in the wall itself allow considerable freedom of movement. At intervals along it stand the high sturdy towers, the *altas torres*, that gave the town its name: how the *madrigal*, or lovesong, came to be added, is anyone's guess.

Within the wall, there appears to be simply another magnificent has-been of Castille. The inhabitants plod about their rustic affairs, incurious and unheeding, past the noble decrepit houses that speak of vanished greatness. But to Madrigal belongs a glory that, even were it reduced to a pile of rubble, can never be taken away: for it was the birthplace of Isabel, daughter of Juan II and Maria of Aragon, wife of Ferdinand, and one of the greatest queens of this or any country.

She had the courage and the resolution of our own Queen Bess; but while the Englishwoman was content to inspire and hearten her troops, Isabel trained and organized hers, planned their campaigns, sold her jewels to feed and pay them, turned up wherever the fighting was thickest, careless of danger, hardship or her own bad health. She was a redoubtable gunner, taking the neglected artillery under her wing, placing the batteries and directing the fire with devastating results. She set up hospitals in the field, hitherto unknown, and imposed on her army a firm discipline, which also came as a novelty. All she undertook went so smoothly and well, her camps were said to resemble Plato's Republic. And yet she was no dragon or battle-axe, nor, like Christina of Sweden, a man absurdly lodged in a female body, but a true woman, gentle and warm of heart. One portrait shows her, the forger of Spain's unity, as a plump maternal lady, without a masculine feature in her face, and with a pensive air, like a housewife pondering whether a guest should go in the Blue or the Yellow Room.

First, then, I set off to see the place where she was born. It was a day of brilliant sun, but so cold that its rays merely raised a steam on the higher roofs and were not felt by those on the ground below. The palace of Juan II of Castille, where he lived with his two wives, first Maria of Aragon, then Isabel of Portugal, was given by the Emperor Carlos V to nuns of the Augustinian order, previously housed beyond the city wall. It is a huge rambling pile, in which today lives a community of twenty-four. Such entrances as I could see had the lifeless air of doors that are never opened. I went into a courtyard forlorn and neglected, with a fig-tree and a vine in the middle and the buildings around seemingly on the point of collapse.

A woman carrying a pail stopped to ask what I wanted, then led me round to where an opening in the arcade admitted us to a precinct, with another massive door and a wooden turnabout. Setting down her pail of mash, the woman briskly rang the bell, remarking, 'Vamos a ver,' as if this procedure sometimes came to naught. After a long pause, a tired old voice within quavered 'Ave Maria Purisima', to which, prompted by a nudge from my companion, I duly replied, 'Sin pecado concebida.' The woman beamed, like a mistress proud of a pupil, and said, 'Mother Turnkey, here is a Frenchwoman to see the palace.' And another pause followed, so long that I ventured to ask if this were an inconvenient hour.

'Wait, wait,' said the voice, and I waited. The woman picked up her pail and went off to feed the hens. Presently there were sounds of a key turning in the door, then silence again. At last the voice said, 'Open, enter.' I went in and found three little old nuns, the Madre Tornera and two sisters, one of whom clutched a giant bell, like those rung in schools, while the other was victim to a dreadful catarrh. Apparently they had been roaming some distant part of the building and had to be rounded up before I was let in. The Madre apparently acted as watchdog as well as turnkey, for she looked me over doubtfully and asked a number of questions about myself, as if a visit to this historic spot were something that needed explaining; but, finally satisfied, she placed me in the care of the nuns and took her leave.

We now set off on our tour of exploration. The nun with the bell incessantly rang it, warning the community of our approach, that they might flee to cover, although the terrific nasal and glottal sounds from her colleague might have served the purpose equally well. It was a measure of the wealth of Spain that neither my guide book nor Turismo had given the convent more than a passing reference; for it was extremely rich in all manner of things, carved ceilings, painted doors, frescoes clear and vivid after centuries, illuminated manuscripts, pictures, furniture and statues. The Royal Chapel was particularly fine, with its broad arched roof, unsupported by a single column, and tombs of the many royal or illustrious women who had lived and died in the cloister. Among its treasures were a St Jeronimo in alabaster, holding a minute crucifix of incredibly fine and perfect detail, and an exquisite figure of St John the Baptist as a boy. There was also a charming Pietas of painted wood, fished out of the sea by a ship's captain and presented by him to King Fernando the Catholic, who passed it on to his two illegitimate daughters, nuns of the convent. Unhappily, nuns can seldom leave well alone and the Virgin later was crowned with a diadem of silver, inlaid with precious stones, which makes her look a fool; but the two little sisters taking me round pointed it out with tremendous pride.

From here we went onto the rooms of Isabel herself on the floor above. On Good Friday one of the stairways leading thither may only be climbed on the knees, the nuns informed me. Like the Santa Scala in Rome, I observed, but they had never heard of that. We passed through one or two small rooms to a wide antechamber, where there was a magnificent crucifix in marble and a collection of interesting portraits of various royal nuns. Many of these were illegitimate, tidied away into the religious life as the custom was: we find two children belonging to Fernando, and doña Juana of Austria, belonging to the Emperor Carlos V, and doña Ana Maria of Austria, belonging to don Juan of Lepanto. They are described as *Hijas naturales*, a pleasanter word than illegitimate, although how any child can be other than natural I have never understood.

There was also the unhappy doña Ana of Austria, rightful daughter of the hero of Lepanto, niece therefore of Philip II, who fell crazily in love with an individual about whom there hangs a mystery to this day. Prince Juan of Portugal had a son Sebastian by his wife and another, Gabriel Espinosa, by the beautiful daughter of a pastry-cook from Madrigal. The two were very much alike, both in their handsome appearance and wild reckless character. When Sebastian succeeded to the Portuguese crown and, deaf to all advice, embarked on a catastrophic military action in Africa, Espinosa went with him; but only one of them returned. After a period this one claimed to be king and declared that it was Espinosa who had died: humiliated by his defeat, he had at first pretended to be the bastard in order to remain *perdu*. This claim was supported by various parties, some from genuine belief, others, like the Venetian republic, from political interest. Philip II did not like it at all and had him arrested and brought to trial. The judge, a kingsman first and last, duly condemned him, although sorely worried by doubt and troubled in his conscience: indeed, as the saying is, 'he never did a day's good after', and very soon died.

Doña Ana appealed to the king for mercy. He, unaware

of her passion, answered kindly but with a firm refusal and the man, whether king or pastry-cook's grandson, was garrotted, quartered, and his head was exposed on a stake. He met his death in a calm dignified manner and, asked on the scaffold if he still maintained he was king, would only reply that God knew the truth. By this time, doña Ana's role in his life had been found out and the king's affection turned to bitter hatred. She was sentenced to perpetual seclusion in her cell, leaving it only to hear Mass on festival days and then under the eye of the 'oldest, gravest nuns', allowed to speak to no one, deprived of all privileges due to her rank, waited on by the common servants of the convent, not selected nuns of noble blood; and, a typical petty meanness of this monarch, she was to have nothing but bread and water all the Fridays of the year.

Had Philip II dealt harshly but justly with an impudent upstart and disturber of the peace, a man 'bajo y vil', as he asserted? Or had he cannily disposed of a dangerous and troublesome rival? Either would fit into his character. The truth of the matter will never now be known, but we may spare a compassionate thought for his lovesick niece. It was amusing to see how the nuns pursed up their lips and looked away at the mention of her name, as if the scandal had but recently broken and somehow reflected on themselves.

Beyond the antechamber was the tiny room, or alcove really, in which the wonder baby was born. 'Such humility!' wheezed the nun with the cold, raising her watery eyes to heaven. Except for a table and crucifix it was left entirely bare, with the instinctive Spanish good taste and simplicity: no cradles, miniatures, dolls, little shoes or other affecting *recuerdos*.

The nuns asked would I care to see the church. As it was open to the public they were not allowed in, but we could take a peep through a grille in one of the apartments, and also visit the little cell where they knelt one by one to receive communion through an opening in the wall. And above this aperture was a precious *relicario*, studded with jewels, and the cell itself was floored with beautiful Talavera tiles: upstairs was a fine *coro*, also with a grille, through which the nuns could feast their eyes on the heavy baroque altar-piece in gold while hearing Mass. It was strange to think of these shabby poor little nuns trotting about all day in their luxurious apartments, and eating their frugal meals under the superbly carved ceiling of what was once the royal audience chamber. I asked if the townspeople came here much, and they replied in chorus with fervour that there was great piety in Madrigal, very great, thanks be to God. And on Good Friday the dead Christ in his shroud and the Mater Dolorosa left the convent and patrolled the streets, amid great popular enthusiasm.

But they were terribly poor, they said, with no dowry or income, and not a penny from the state, despite the care they took of the precious monuments.

How, then, did they live?

They pointed through a window to a patch of disconsolate vegetables in the garden below. On those, they said, and from the fees of a little school they ran. But it was a very little school, and not every child could pay.

I would have liked to know more of their life and doings, how they passed the day, what they talked about among themselves, what were the dreams that came at night, and what on earth they taught the children. St John of the Cross says in his *Consejos* that nobody should entertain such a wish, not even a professed nun or monk. 'Never be concerned either by word or by thought in what takes place within a community nor with its individuals, not wishing to know either its good things or its bad, or its conditions,' he exhorts us roundly. But Juan de la Cruz was a saint and his counsels those of perfection.

In the middle of the palace was a noble *patio*, with a big well and a tangle of neglected shrubs and bushes. The nuns said it was a most delicious place in summer, but now . . . vaya! How did I find the weather today?

'On the chilly side,' I answered: in fact, I was slowly

becoming a block of ice and no longer had any sensation at all in either hands or feet.

'Fresquito, sí!' cried the nun with the bell, as if that were just the word for it. 'And it has been thus for weeks. The Sister here has a cold in the head from it.'

The Sister bore the statement out with a couple of seismic sneezes.

'Bud id is bery healdhy here, doo,' she said in a drowning voice. 'No wub is eber really ill.'

When I told them I must be going, they smiled shyly and asked if I were *contenta*. I was *contentísima*, not least to be hurrying out of this ice-box into the sun, while the brave little creatures returned to their arctic cell or tepid vegetable stew.

Opposite the convent was another large building, which turned out to be a Hospital founded by María of Aragon in 1443 and today a dilapidated museum, used for nothing. I did not go in, for even the local panegyrist found little to say about it, and besides I was intent on regaining the tropical warmth of the posada and sitting down to one of its square, or rather octagonal, meals. But the way to it led past the parish church of St Nicholas, where Isabel was 'born again to the life of grace', as a Falange plaque expressed it; and I went in, for a look at the baptistry. This, like her nursery, had been left entirely bare, containing no more than a massive stone font with fluted sides and the heavy wooden candlestick, painted in goldleaf, with imitation candle, that seems indispensable to national monuments.

There was a requiem Mass going on at the time, the priest in black and gold singing his part in a reedy pipe, while the responses came beautifully from a lad in rough workaday clothes. The women sat together at the front of the church, the men at the back, as in parts of Ireland. Outside, waited a motor-hearse with a silver angel blowing a trumpet at each corner of the roof, and the name *Soledad* (loneliness) emblazoned on its side. Even in this remote *pueblo*, evidently, the ornate hearses drawn by black steeds with funereal trappings and plumes, for which the poor

112

used to scrimp and save from their youth onward, were out of fashion.

In the afternoon I went for a walk, accompanied by the *posada* Alsatian. From the way he flew about, up every alley, into every door and after every stray fowl, I inferred that he was rarely off the chain. To avoid scandal, I led him out of the town and walked for several miles along the road to Avila; but no matter how far we went, everything looked the same, flat, brown, and limitless as the sea. Approaching vehicles climbed into view nose first, just as ships climb over the horizon, and the few scattered *poblaciones* lay about like vessels for ever becalmed. It was an odd kind of country walk, with never a stream or wood or hill to tempt one off the road, nothing but rough stony ground broken here and there with patches of cultivation.

Presently the sun went down, the sky took on the dull red of cooling metal, and the cold became intense. The Alsatian's transports being somewhat calmed, we returned to the comparative liveliness of Madrigal. Though hardly beautiful, the town did possess its own weird charm, with the remnants of grandeur rubbing shoulders with the squalors of today. Near St Nicholas was an imposing edifice, built in the eighteenth century, now both the prison and a school, a peculiar combination somehow calling to mind Mr P. G. Wodehouse's inventor, with his pencil sharpener cum mousetrap. And another, not far off, was put up in the reign of Carlos IV and Luisa of Borbón, to help the *jornaleros*, or casual day-to-day labourers, an unhappy class which until quite recently has always lived near starvation level. How in that day this desirable end was to be achieved, we are not told, but the first move of Spaniards with a project is invariably to run up a grandiose building: not infrequently, it is the last one as well.

For a long long time, as the town sank further and further into decadence, the inhabitants consoled themselves with the belief that enormous earthenware pots, full of gold, were immured in various houses of the departed nobility. One lady still remembers a 'treasure hunt' in her youth, when some redoubtable boy with a pickaxe set about a wall in her own dwelling and, to the frantic excitement of all, actually uncovered a heavy clay jar. It proved to contain books, immensely old and no doubt of great value; but such was the disappointment that no importance was attached to the find whatever, and the books were used as domestic fuel.

This was quite of a piece with the normal Spanish attitude to cultural, as opposed to material, riches. I myself once saw a window with a missing pane replaced by a fine old picture, and have often, in monastery libraries, come on rare illuminated parchments bundled away and left to the mice. Alonso de Encinas, who tells the lady's story in his booklet on Madrigal, is able to cap it with one of his own: his task was made difficult by a paucity of information, he tells us, due to an official of the Ayuntamiento having sold the contents of the archives for a song, as 'papelote', or waste paper.

The local amplifiers, fixed here and there at strategic points, now burst into full cry with a record of the Singing Nun. Fleeing from her in one direction, you ran slap into her advancing from another: the whole *pueblo* echoed with her winsome caterwaul, and I scuttled back to the *posada*, preceded by the Alsatian, tail between legs.

I went into the salon to write some notes, and found a log fire blazing on the hearth, despite the fact that the house was already centrally heated to oven temperature. The handsome white-haired manageress was sitting there chatting to a stranger, whom I took to be a newly arrived guest; but it soon emerged that he was a doctor, and she consulting him, so I hastily got up to go.

'Sientase, sientase,' the hostess called out, affably. 'No se preocupa.'

Yes, she continued, she had shocking pains in her back and legs and no small inconvenience with her bladder. (I betray no confidence, as the information was available to anyone within earshot.) What with the pain and the necessity for constantly getting up, she hardly closed an eye at night. The doctor groaned in sympathy, but said it was to be expected in this cold: many of his patients were similarly afflicted.

Their climate was among the healthiest in Spain, he went on, I think for my benefit, as he raised his voice a little; but certainly the winters were cold. And the summers hot, moaned the Señora: ay, qué calor! And the terrible winds of spring! One could hardly stand upright in them. But the climate was none the less agreeable, the doctor insisted, stoutly defending it as a piece of personal property; and for his part he never felt really well anywhere else.

'You have never been to my tierra!' the patient cracked back.

There now ensued a wrangle about their respective *tierras*, neither affected by the arguments of the other or even listening to them, which the Señora at last cut short by ringing the bell.

'Let us all take a copita,' she proposed.

The *copitas* arrived, including one for me, and the conversation turned to the beauties and glories of Madrigal, until the Señora suddenly attacked the doctor again.

'So there is nothing you can do for me,' she said dolefully.

'I never said that,' he replied, hurt. 'I merely said your condition was "regular".' With that, he wrote out a number of prescriptions, among them one for a *supositorio* – is there anything in the world from a sore throat to a sprained ankle for which Spanish doctors will not prescribe a *supositorio?* – and bowed himself out.

The Señora contemplated the sheaf of papers in her hand with a look both satisfied and rueful. 'He is a very able doctor,' she confided, 'but, I imagine, related to the chemist.'

There seemed no comment I could usefully make, and I made none.

12

My first night at the *posada* I had slept straight through, *de un tirón*, and concluded from this that here was an idyllically tranquil resting-place. It must have been due to exhaustion, however, after the pandemonium in honour of the Prince of Peace the night before: for on the second, while there were no crashes or splintering glass or yells, the *posada* plumbing maintained a steady blare that was every whit as effective.

I had determined on visiting the great castle of Coca next day, via Medina del Campo and Olmedo. The night porter was to call me at seven and, for safety's sake, buzzed a long piercing trill on the telephone at six. At half past seven he appeared at my door, to insist that I leave forthwith. It seemed premature, to catch a bus a few hundred yards away at eight; but I saw the point of it when I got outside and found that the streets were wholly unlit. Cursing, I stumbled blindly over the cobbles and through the middens, past St Nicholas to the *puerta* Medina, at which the bus would stop. A great throng was assembled there, but mercifully not all were travelling: some were seeing their friends and relations off, with a great deal of kissing and embracing, while others had merely come to watch the bus depart, no doubt the peak of their daily round.

When it arrived and we got in, it looked at first as if all the seats were taken. This was simply due to the fact that each occupant sat on the outer one, with his luggage beside him next to the window. To spread one's belongings out in this way to prevent incursion is an old Spanish custom, leading, as now, to battles which, however, once lost leave no hard feelings behind. The woman I tackled swore that the place beside her was *ocupada*, its owner having just slipped out for a cup of coffee: I countered the gambit with one of my own, asking permission to sit in it until he returned: sulkily, she moved her cases, bags and parcels away and let me pass; and by the time the bus moved off, all was forgiven and we chatted away together like old friends.

Slowly the sun came up. The tremendous plain, so drab and dingy the day before, was white with frost this morning as far as the eye could see, and sparkling in the rosy light. At Medina, half frozen, I went to a workman's bar for brandy and coffee. There were, the proprietor said, no buses to Olmedo in the winter, but there was a train leaving in ten minutes time. As one can never be absolutely sure that such statements are false, I drank my breakfast up and rushed to the station. The train, a two-coach autocar, left an hour later. A thick mist gathered, turning the sun to a dull red ball and the whole scene, as we rattled along, was like some impressionist painting of winter, the passing locomotives spouting plumes of white smoke towards the woolly grey sky and here and there the flames of wayside fires casting a red glow on the frosty ground.

Frozen again when we reached Olmedo, I took a second repast of brandy and coffee at a little hovel behind the station. For all its poverty-stricken appearance, there was a television going full tilt and giving the football news. It was followed with strained attention by a ragged crew, who shushed indignantly, like an audience at the London Opera, if anyone spoke or noisily moved a chair. The *dueña* was poorly dressed, but neat, and with a very pleasant air, so pleasant that I took courage and asked if I might use her *retrete:* at which her smile vanished, giving way to a look of embarrassed alarm.

'Retrete!' she echoed, as if I had called for a Turkish bath.

Yes, *retrete:* for there seemed to be none in the station itself.

She pondered a while, with a careworn look, then led the way across the yard to a lean-to stable, full of mouldering straw, and pointed to one corner of it. 'There,' she said, in a low shamed voice. 'How about that?'

I next walked on to Olmeda itself, a good ten minutes away. A friend had assured me it boasted a fine restaurant, quite famous among motorists travelling the region, and I stepped out smartly, being altogether famished. My informant was the very man who had so warmly recommended the dire residencia in Madrid, and why I still took his word for anything is hard to understand. The fine restaurant was a seedy pull-up for lorries, heavy with the fumes of unrefined olive oil; and I broke my fast with a couple of eggs fried in this, the yolks to the consistency of sponge, the whites like a frame of slimy rubber, bread like a brick and coffee that reminded me of nothing at all.

I then set forth to hire a taxi to bring me to Coca, but as luck would have it, every single one in the *pueblo* that same morning, by a strange coincidence, *¡qué raro!*, had broken down. Then a kindly citizen, overhearing my lamentations, offered to take me there himself, if he might have half an hour to pull his car together. I spent the time wandering about the town, which seemed in the very last stage of dissolution, with great fissures in the buildings, as after an earthquake, peeling walls, and the very vanes on the churches bent awry, presumably by the *tornados* of spring. The minute the half hour was up, I hastened back to where I had left the obliging citizen, but could see no more of him than his boots, protruding from under the vehicle. This was a jalopy in the good rustic tradition, with a cracked windscreen, the inside door-handles broken off, impeding rapid exit in the probable emergency, gashes in the upholstery and a kind of incompatibility of body and bonnet, as if they had come together by chance.

118

'Momentito!' came in a muffled voice from the owner; and although the *momentito* extended itself to another half hour, when finally he wriggled out, he got the engine running, a triumph of human ingenuity over mechanics.

We passed through long miles of sandy waste and thickets of pines, which looked like umbrellas blown inside out. When we left the *carretera* for the track leading up to the castle, we encountered such knolls and gulches in it that we might have been driving across open country. The castle itself, crowning a hill, was stupendous viewed from some way off, one of the finest examples of Mudejar in Spain and a masterpiece of Moorish building. Wherever the Moor went in Spain, his doings were beneficial. He created splendid palaces, temples, monuments, gardens, he transformed arid wastes into regions of plenty by the use of irrigation, he brought medical skills far beyond anything known to Europe and, as a conqueror, showed himself chivalrous and humane, in sorry contrast to the Spaniard. Yet the expulsion of the Moors is regarded as the glory of Spain and celebrated with pious fervour to this day. But this same castle on closer inspection turned out to be one more victim of restoration. Spain really is being restored within an inch of her life: no matter how well and tastefully the work is done, there is a deadness in it, as in the lifted face of a woman. A ruin will often stir the imagination, a restored building never. All round the courtyards was flood-lighting gear, which added to the feeling of spuriousness. But there were marvellous views of the country from every corner of the ramparts, the sun having driven the early mist away and casting a glow on the two rivers that meet here, on the boskies round the village of Coca and over the great prairie.

My driver's willingness to hazard his moribund car over this rough course was now explained: he had some private business in the locality and drove away, with smoke belching from his exhaust, while I continued to explore the castle alone. No guards or caretakers were to be found, or any signs of occupation apart from bundles of wood, neatly tied, as if the old fortress today was nothing more than a forester's depot. I climbed down steep narrow flights of stairs to the dungeons beneath, but as I approached the entrance to them a couple of mastiffs rushed out snarling, and I retired in haste. Evidently something in the keeps had been left in their charge, for they made no attempt to follow and even wagged their tails when I looked down at them from the safety of the rampart. There was something weird and romantic about it all, the huge silent building, open to the world and quite forsaken but for the guardian dogs below and the jackdaws wheeling around the turrets overhead.

Presently the car came limping up the hill, the engine coughing and smoke pouring now from the bonnet as well as from the exhaust. My friend had collected four burly companions for the homeward trip and we set off at a funeral pace, squeezed together like chickens for market and choked by the fumes, while the *dueño* alternately reviled and wheedled the car, as if it had been a recalcitrant mule.

'She has her moods, this máquina,' he told us, 'but I'll get you there, don't worry.'

Against all likelihood, he eventually did so, as complacent and proud as if he had won the Monte Carlo rally. He refused so much as the price of a drink from me, declaring the pleasure had all been his, wrung my hand repeatedly and wished me *buen viaje*. At the pull-in for car men, they told me there was no train now that would get to Medina in time for the Madrigal bus, but a lorry was leaving at any minute, almost any minute, as soon as the driver finished his game of chess. The youth in question, snubnosed and bullheaded as Sancho Panza, did not look like much of a chess man, nor was he. His moves were so extraordinary, I feared they might be devilish deep, resulting in one of those endless games that champions play; but a very few of them brought the game to a close, and he was ready to start. In Spain there is a kind of persistent luck, which balances and atones for her organization, so that no one need ever despair.

The youth, whose name was Jesús, cheerfully consented

120

to take me with him. Despite the defeat at chess, he was in
high spirits and they steadily rose along the way since, like
Borrow's Antonio of Finisterra, he paused to 'refresh' wherever he got the chance. His grounds for celebration were
two, he said, the completion of his military service and the
finding of a job just four days later. It was the happy conclusion to a tale of woe, for were there any justice in the
world he should never have been in the Army at all. As the
only son of a widow he was exempt, and had lived in peace,
waited on by his mother hand and foot and basking in the
envy of his conscript friends. But then, unaccountably, perverse and capricious like all females, she had upped and
married again. Likewise unaccountably, the husband had
failed to offer Jesús a home. He was left to fend for himself,
running the ex-widow's shop and doing his own chores like
a girl. This was bad enough, but worse was to follow. In
due course the Army heard of the marriage and called him
up, a brutal and, as he saw it, completely wanton act.

'They exempted me because my father was dead,' he rea-
soned. 'And he still is. I don't see where my mother came
in.'

'I think the Army exempted you so that you could pro-
vide for her,' I said.

'But she always provided for *me*,' Jesús objected. 'No, I
think it was because my father had died.'

'Certainly. Because he was no longer there to support
her.'

'She always supported *him*,' said Jesús in triumph. 'She is
a mujer fuerte. Now she is running her husband's affairs,
and he has nothing to say.'

'The Army couldn't know that.'

The Army knows nothing at all,' was the sombre reply.
'It has no brain, no heart, no commonsense. How can an
orphan cease to be an orphan? Barbaridad!'

Nevertheless the Army had taught him to drive; and
during his term he made friends with another conscript,
whose father had given him his present job. And a cousin
bought the shop. Really, things had turned out for the best,

121

but it was no thanks to any of the parties involved; and through his present euphoria there fitfully showed the resentments of a much wronged man.

Medina del Campo, or City of the Plain, possesses the great castle where Isabel the Catholic died in 1504, having moved there in 1479. They were restless characters, the royalties of that age, constantly moving house or building palaces, only to give them away again. This one, with its pinkish walls and fine turreted tower, serenely crowning a hillock, I had often admired from train windows on the way to Valladolid, and always hoped to visit; but luck was out. Today a boarding-school for girls, it must have been shut for the Christmas holiday, as no one came in response to my knocking and ringing. A TV aerial was the only sign of its being used at all, and the place was quite given up to the jackdaws, who screeched indignantly at me from the tower, wagging their grey heads and fretfully plunging in and out of their holes.

Apart from the castle, Medina had little to recommend it. Even in its heyday as a king's residence and busy trading centre, it was despised by the courtiers who had to live there. They nicknamed it City of the Dirt and groaned at the weather, and the Bishop of Mondoñedo wrote sarcastically in 1532, 'It hath a river that is so deep and dangerous, that geese in summer go over it dry-footed'. Its decline was not slow and gradual, as with most Castilian townships, but abrupt: in 1520 over nine hundred of its houses were burned by the *comuneros*, peasants revolting against the monarchy, and it never quite recovered. What was left was repeatedly sacked and pillaged by the French at the time of the Peninsular War, and now its only distinctive feature is its position, more or less equidistant from Avila, Segovia, Salamanca and Palencia.

The evening bus to Madrigal was crowded again with peasants, the men all drunk, a state of affairs to which I was becoming inured. One of them, with tears in his eyes, repeatedly showed me a hole in his new jacket, burned by someone's cigar in the bus that morning. The talk grew racy and wild: to begin with, I understood roughly one word in three, then as it warmed up, none at all. The women sizzled their disapproval, with the sharp incisive hiss formerly used to summon waiters, to which the carousers paid not the slightest attention. It is sad how a people's character melts away, when the basis of it has gone. The qualities that once marked the Spaniard out, the decency, frugality, stoicism, pride, were the response to bitter privations; and these were now removed, like props kicked from under a vessel, leaving her in headlong downward career.

The lights of Madrigal twinkled on the far horizon. At last we were there, and with a great deal of shouting, the revellers climbed unsteadily down. From the tower of San Nicholas came the mew of the Singing Nun. I floundered through mud and darkness to the *posada*, where some jovial stranger bought me a drink for Navidad.

That evening after dinner I read some of the Falange newspapers offered by the hotel for the public enjoyment. There was an article severely criticizing the *viviendas*, or working-class flats, which the Government is throwing up all over the country. The walls of the *viviendas*, the writer declared, were much too thin, making for heat in summer and cold in winter and, further, constituting a threat to the privacy of families, since everything could be heard through them. To what extent any Spaniard values privacy, is something I have never been able to determine; but the amusing part of these strictures was, they applied equally to the luxurious and expensive *posada* itself.

In the night that followed, this was made abundantly clear. The plumbing and heating installations growled away as before, and every sigh and moan of the Señora, suffering from her legs at the far end of the passage, was plainly heard. Worse, there now was a man in the room next to mine and whenever he turned on the light, it was like a pistol shot in my ear. At a quarter to two, he telephoned to his wife, long distance, inquiring minutely after the health and conduct of each of his seven children. At last, the philoprogenitive monster reached an end and I sank back on my pillows in relief; but he had not done. He next rang up his mother, also long distance, to pass on the information received from his wife and to ask tenderly about mama's own household. I hated the man. I could have killed him. My snarls of rage grew louder and louder, but he was quite unmoved, indeed, probably unconscious of them.

In the morning the Señora expressed the hope that I had enjoyed a tranquil repose.

'A nice quiet place here, no?' she asked. There was a gleam of something in her eye, but it was hard to say what.

13

The next trip was to be to Guadalupe, over the Sierra de Gredos and taking in La Vera, a pleasant fertile region along the southern slopes of that formidable range. For this, it was necessary first to go back to Avila, a journey almost as dull by day as in darkness. The only village of any note was Fontiveros, and that merely because St John of the Cross was born there. In itself the *pueblo* was seedy and ramshackle, living apparently in a permanent doze with the blinds all drawn and hardly a soul astir. It is curious that the saint, whose finest poems were all in praise of the beauties of nature, should have passed his early years in a land so devoid of any charm.

Avila now had a weary dishevelled look, the party over, the money all spent and no one inclined for effort of any description. In the afternoon I left for the parador nacional de Gredos, being the sole passenger in the bus, for a welcome change. The journey took two and a half hours, and as it drew near its end the landscape grew steadily wilder and more desolate, with great stretches of snow-covered forest and numerous rapid streams. A cruel wind rushed through the mountain tops, not howling or shrieking like winds in the plain, but with a deep reverberating rumble like the roar of cannon.

The parador stood about 1600 metres above the sea, all by itself, a grim flinty building that looked more like a fortified keep than a hotel. Inside, however, all was bustle and animation. The salon was crammed with people, drinking, playing cards or gazing with fond delight at their shrieking children, while the tele bugled away in a corner. I had expected the other guests to be lean tough hunting or climbing types, but they turned out to be all of the Franco class, newly rich and eager to impress. One lady sat by the fire, wrapped in a fur stole, explaining with a martyred air that the room was colder than she was accustomed to. A fat young man in riding clothes recounted an experience of the afternoon, when the stallion he rode had taken the bit between its teeth and shot away like the wind. And there was an assortment of women in smart little dresses, with dyed hair and rattling bracelets, who talked indefatigably, keeping a parroty eye on everyone else meanwhile. What had induced them all to leave their cosy flats for this bleak solitary mountain, miles from anywhere, with nothing to do but what they could have equally well have done at home? There was something bizarre about it, as if a comedy of suburban life were filming in sets designed for *The Call of the Wild*, or similar work.

The wind roared angrily through the night but dropped at dawn, and the day broke soft and mild. Setting out to explore, I was privileged to see the fat young horseman mounting his steed. It was a sorry nag, of the kind one sees in the bullring, and stood with hanging head, apparently fast asleep; but once the cavalier was in the saddle, it flattened its ears and started hurriedly walking backwards round and round the yard, while the rider anxiously begged it to stop.

'Shorten the reins, señor,' said the groom, a spare little man with the sardonic expression of grooms all over the world, 'and keep your hands and heels down.' For the youth's hands were level with his chin, and his feet were about to lose the stirrups. 'Show him who is the master!' he added unkindly.

'I can't!' was the piteous reply. 'Oh, catch hold of him, do!'

Musing as often before upon the gulf between aspiration

and performance, fancy and fact, I left them to it and went down into the forest. It was a beautiful walk, with the breeze singing in the branches, soft green moss underfoot. little brooks rustling here and there, and the stillness of living trees all round. Now and again in a clearing there were cattle, fat and sleek, with bells round their necks: vast rainbows appeared, spanning the distant peaks: light showers of rain, the drops sparkling in the sun, would suddenly fall, then as suddenly cease.

I went on and on, in a wide circular sweep, and never met a soul until I reached the glade leading up to the parador. Here, a little way ahead, was the horseman again, indulging in stranger antics than ever. I could not immediately think what he was about; but as I drew near it became apparent that his naf was trying to canter home, while he was doing his utmost to prevent it, so that he looked for all the world like a man on a rocking-horse. Such peacocks are Spanish men, however, that on noting he had an audience he threw caution to the winds and, giving the horse its head, cantered bravely towards a jump across the path that was fully twelve inches high. Unhappily he muffed it and knocked the whole thing down, sweeping on to dismount, or rather fall off, in the yard and thankfully surrender the mustang to his groom. Then he strode into the parador, where I found him in the bar, slapping his boot with his whip and talking horses in hearty manly tones, as befitted a caballero.

Now the wind was rising again, the sky turned feathery and dark and snow began to fall, the huge white flakes whirling endlessly down past the windows to settle on the forest far beneath. Frequent dramatic changes of weather are usual in these parts, and a couple of hours later the sky cleared and the sun came out, although it was freezing hard. After luncheon I slid down the road to Navarredonda, a little *pueblo* some two miles away. One solitary vehicle was travelling up it, a lorry, with two smiling unshaven men in the cabin: they naturally had to stop and ask who I was, what doing, where from and whither bound, only to find

127

when at last they had done that their wheels refused to turn on the glassy slope. I pulled branches of broom from the wayside and strewed the ground until they got off, which they did waving farewell and shouting *piropos* in the best of humour.

Navarredonda hardly repaid the effort of reaching it, for it was as desolate a spot as I ever saw. Half the houses were boarded up, either to keep the cold out or because the owners had fled, and the church had an abandoned air, like those churches burned or sacked in the Civil War and never put to rights. Moreover, it was doubtful if I could ever get up the hill again without the help of a ski-lift or windlass. I went along the Avenida del Generalísimo, a forlorn and squalid thoroughfare, hoping to buy a walking stick and accompanied by a tiny old woman, who kept exclaiming Qué calor! amid shrieks of laughter. There were but two little shops in the village and neither had a stick. The proprietor of the first alleged he had sold the last one that morning, he of the second apologized for not keeping them but suggested postcards or a bottle of brandy instead. That gave me a happy idea, and I inquired of the tiny woman if Navarredonda boasted a bar.

'Two!' she answered proudly: 'one at each end of the town.' But although she had lived here all her life she had never been in either, and knew nothing about them. She conducted me to that which was nearer and left me at the door, declining an invitation to venture inside. The establishment was more like a miniature barn than a café and had a pleasantly rural atmosphere about it. Three black bulls were rubbing their necks on the wall, making the bells round them clang like a fire-engine; and over a leaping bonfire in the yard four men were gravely burning the bristles off a pig, each holding a limb, twisting the heavy carcase this way and that, their craggy faces lit by the flames, a vivid and homely scene like some old Flemish painting.

Inside a dozen men or so were clustered round a small iron stove in the middle of the room. If they were surprised or shocked to see a woman enter they gave no sign of it, but greeted me with much civility and at once made way at the fire, the dueño removing his beret and asking what he should serve. With things thus comfortably set, as if on a cue the smiling lorry-men walked in and hailed me like a dear, long-lost relation, so easy are human contacts in Spain. The whole matter of my rescue work with the broom was thoroughly gone over and *copitas* freely poured, for none of which I was allowed to pay. Better still when the time came to go, they would not hear of my struggling home on foot but packed me into the lorry, declaring that nothing would please them more than a second cold and hazardous drive to the summit. I did not argue long, for it is undeniably simpler to slide down a hill than up it; and off we went, the afternoon ending happily and unexpectedly, as so many afternoons had done before.

A profound peace reigned over the parador. It had made itself already felt at luncheon, when I had put it down to the snow, which muffles the noise of the world and has a muting effect on people's very voices. Now the hush was greater then ever and the true reason for it emerged: in the course of the day the Spanish guests had all departed, their places being taken by foreigners, mostly French. A few of these were sitting by the fire, conversing in what seemed to be undertones but was really the accepted European pitch. They were taking Spain to pieces with good-humoured contempt, saying nothing but what was true and what I often said myself; and still, with the jealousy of an old Spanish hand, I felt annoyed. It was their misfortune, not their fault, if travelling prosaically by car from one parador to the next they missed the real joys of the country, but they too clearly never supposed there might be any. All reduced itself to things that fell apart or did not work, to requests that were ignored or improperly carried out, to luggage or laundry that was mislaid and to food that tasted all the same: the catalogue went on and on, to the accompaniment of ironic little French chuckles.

While they talked, the tele had been muttering to itself, as if in indignation, and presently, its patience doubtless exhausted, it began to bellow with all the power at its command. The shadowy figures flitting across the screen disappeared in a sort of waterfall, that moved horizontally rather than vertically, and was utterly blinding to watch.

'Ah ça alors! Non!' said one of the company, pouting. Leaping up, he set about the apparatus without the least result, good or bad, then gave a vehement tug to the service bell, which came away in his hand. 'Incroyable!'

A man came in with a basket of logs just then and was excitedly urged to intervene; but he replied that the disturbance was due to the snow and there was no remedy for bad weather.

But you can turn it off, voyons!

No: for some technical reason that was impossible also. Calmly he placed the logs on the fire and withdrew, while the tele burst into maniac laughter and the waterfall gave way to a blizzard of dots and dashes. Shrugging and pulling faces, the French trooped out in a body, whereupon the apparatus, as if only waiting for that, immediately held its peace.

A big blond man looked across at me with a smile. 'A very Spanish instrument,' he remarked. 'I think it must have understood.' And it seemed very likely too. The blows of Spanish installations fall with such diabolical precision, it is hard to believe they are not thought out. The big man chatted easily on until it was time for dinner. He was a business man from Holland, travelling alone, and enjoying himself immensely. Tourist though he was, and only a short while in the country, he had found out a number of useful things to know. 'This people shows itself to friends,' he said. 'If you complain and grumble, it hides itself away. And the faults that visitors find don't worry me at all. Those things they find lacking, I can have at home, and better. Do you know what strikes me here the most? The freedom. At home, in my free country, in theory you can do everything, in practice, nothing. Here, it is precisely the other way round.'

In truth, this glorious freedom is one of Spain's abiding

charms: the Spaniards themselves do not know how lucky they are, and take it all for granted. And I admired the Dutchman for tumbling to it so fast, having myself realized it but slowly, after long experience.

Meanwhile the snow came steadily down, and all through that evening and the night. There is an old carol, two lines of which run *Snow was falling, snow on snow Snow on snow on snow*, and these had always struck me as verging on the repetitious. Now they seemed a perfect description, as hour after hour the noiseless downpour continued. By morning, the landscape was transfigured, its every feature swallowed up in the vast glittering whiteness. I went down into the forest by the same route as the day before, but constantly straying from it and floundering waist-high in drifts. There was no singing from the trees now, their branches too heavily laden to stir, and there was hardly a sound at all but what came from the mountain streams, purling downward, wriggling black serpents against the white. Now and then a bank of snow toppled off its perch with a noise like a deep sigh, or fell on me with a gentle thud; and sometimes the trees parted a little, showing a patch of deep blue sky or dove-coloured cloud far above.

A couple of hours or so brought me to the valley, to find that I was lost. A plain granite cross, set up on a huge boulder, with a dead wreath round it, marked the Falangist victory of 1939, for the wretches drag it into everything, even an apolitical forest. I had not passed the monument the day before, and therefore must have parted company with the track; and rather than risk myself in the forest again, I ploughed strenuously across open country, often swimming rather than walking, losing shoes and digging them out with frozen hands and, by the time the parador was reached, having all the air of a mobile snowman. For half an hour after I went indoors, I was completely blind, with nothing before my eyes but a blank screen of purple.

The beauty of the Sierra, the crisp biting air, the wonderful peace after the hurlyburly of the plains, were so exhilarating that I would gladly have stayed there longer; but I was anxious to see La Vera before going on to Guadalupe for New Year's Eve. After luncheon I drove down to the cross-roads, where a coach for Arenas de San Pedro was due to pass. Once more I had reckoned without Spain and once more it all turned out for the best. There was no coach to Arenas that afternoon, it simply failed to come. The roads were not blocked or anything of that kind, it was the coach's personal decision. After fretting by the wayside until hope was gone, I went into the Fonda del Obispo to drink anis and ruminate. For all its name, the *fonda* was not a place where any bishop would gladly stay: rather, it was such as don Quixote might have stumbled on, with its flagged floors, low heavily-beamed ceilings, sacks of meal, mounds of firewood and, in a corner where the family now were eating, strings of sausages, onions and garlic hung overhead. There was a powerful reek of crude olive oil, mingled with another, which I diagnosed as tom-cat. The landlady, a stout cheerful bewhiskered woman, left her dinner and told me the thing to do was stand on the highway and thumb a lift. Otherwise I should have to spend the night there, and that would not be suitable. I would have had no objection to it, for there was something attractive about the place, the homely lodging with the river tearing along past the door and the snowy mountains beyond; but she was adamant that it would not do, and even called in a man from chopping logs to bear her out. And so I fell to pacing up and down the road again, thanking God for the warm sun and wondering how I should fare once it set.

Car after car went by. Sometimes an owner responded to signals with a kindly wave of the hand in passing, which was worse than being ignored. Presently a smart new van, marked Official Service: Sanitary Department, drew up and the two men inside engaged in a polite little struggle. One of them, who had evidently been given a lift, offered a hundred-peseta note to the driver, who proudly refused it. The passenger insisted, with no better result. The driver wished it understood that Government vehicles did not ply for hire, nor did a gentleman accept payment for merely obliging another: this dialogue continued until both points were fully established and the official could trouser the money with honour satisfied and dignity intact.

I asked the public-spirited fellow where he was bound for, but unhappily it was to Navarredonda, on urgent affairs of state.

'This gentleman goes to Arenas too,' he said. 'I would gladly take you both, but the people yonder await me. They have been urging me to visit them for weeks.'

He drove off and left the pair of us to pace up and down, shivering and blowing on our fingers. At last a real taxi came along, containing three passengers, who philosophically squeezed themselves together, bidding us join them and welcome. The reason for such friendly behaviour soon was clear, for the canny *taxista* was covering the route of the defaulting coach, setting down and taking up and doing a very brisk trade. At one moment there were nine souls in the car, a pig and some fowls in the boot, and baggage enough on top to swing us drunkenly from side to side. Uncomfortable as we were, the drive was beautiful, over the winding mountain road with magnificent views of the Sierra on one hand, on the other a wide rich valley of terraced orchards and olive groves, the river weaving in and out among them like some enormous snake. The air grew warmer and warmer, until even my Spanish travelling companions wanted the windows open, and by the time we reached Arenas, barely twenty-five miles from the frozen uplands of Gredos, it was soft and balmy as an evening in May.

I left my luggage at a hostel and went on tour in the lovely old town while still there was light. The contrast with the frozen heights of the morning was such that Arenas might have been in another country. Orange trees with the fruit still on were in every little garden and women, lightly clad, sang as they washed their clothes in the river. Everything here was lively and cheerful and bustling. Over the Gothic bridge beyond the *plaza mayor* was an open workshop where men were making tables and chairs by lamplight: near that, a sawmill was hard at work, the new-cut timber giving off a delicious smell. The river wound placidly away to the horizon, losing itself in dark woods above which towered the peaks of Gredos, pink in the dying sun. Men trotted by on mules and called out a friendly *Adiós!* Dogs barked mildly, wagging their tails to show they meant no harm. From the old granite church of the Assumption came the hollow note of a bell, tolling for somebody's death. The sky turned green, then indigo, and the stars came out one by one.

At the end of this long charming walk I dropped into the first restaurant I saw, Los Monteros, which proved unexpectedly good. I was their only customer, however, and so glad were they to see one that a *copita* was promptly brought, with the compliments of the *dueño*. The waiter told me business was slack – as I had already surmised – and, as for foreigners, he rarely saw one and had no idea of foreign ways, likes and dislikes. He plainly thought that here was a chance to learn, for every time he removed a dish he canvassed my opinion of it in the closest detail. Sad to say, in all innocence, I left him under a serious misapprehension. I was eating leg of baby lamb when a famished dog slunk in and looked at me with a piteous appeal there was no resisting: I threw him the bones: a quick crunch or two and they were gone, and the dog as well. Soon afterwards the waiter returned and was eagerly asking how the Señora had enjoyed her *cordero* when his eye fell on the empty plate and the words fairly froze on his lips. From his look it was clear he supposed I had swallowed the bones myself: in the unsophisticated *pueblos* of Spain, foreigners are believed capable of anything. Explaining matters would not have helped, for no Spanish diner-out thinks of feeding a dog, and he would merely have put me down as insane. I therefore left it at that, with him, in sore distress of mind, anxiously keeping watch from the doorway for the rest of the meal, as if expecting me to polish off the china and cutlery.

After dinner, night having fallen, I went back through the

narrow twisting streets, with their cobble stones and old iron lamps, to the hostel. The concierge at the parador had warned me it was *regular*, or nothing special, and he had somewhat understated. A woman and her daughter, both dressed in black, owned the place, but it was ruled oppressively by the younger female's two appalling children: her husband had taken to his heels. Banks of paper flowers met the eye at every turn: the bed was lumpy and the sheets damp: on this particular day, no hot water was to be procured. But I was too pleased with Arenas as a whole to worry about trifles, and in any case was extremely tired. I fell into the bed, which received my weight with a resentful twang, and slept like a baby till morning.

Early next morning, after a cup of what seemed to be melted coffee-blancmange and a few stale biscuits, I went down to the *plaza mayor* and hired a taxi. Before setting out along La Vera, we first drove to the burial place of St Peter Alcántara, from whom the township Arenas took its name. This friar was one of the closest friends and advisers of St Teresa, and a man of great and uncomfortable holiness. For forty years he slept only an hour and a half at night, and then sitting down, his cell being too narrow to allow of anything else: he never covered his head in the hottest sun or the heaviest rain, went barefoot, wore sackcloth next to his skin, as tight as possible, and usually ate once every three days, although sometimes it would be once in eight. After his death in 1562 he appeared on three occasions to St Teresa, at the third putting heart into her when the devil was plotting against the foundation of San José.

The Sanctuary was charmingly placed on a hill, with a background of pines, and overlooking the town a mile away. San Pedro's tomb was very small, a humble affair for a Spanish saint, and surrounded by a thicket of brambles. The friar who escorted me said that once, attacked by a sudden temptation, San Pedro threw himself on these by way of penance, whereupon the thorns were miraculously removed and never grew again. He broke off a spray and pressed it on me, with earnest entreaty that I should verify the truth of his words for myself. The brambles are a large family, however, and this species looked like one of those that are thornless from the start. It would not have done to say so, for to friars and nuns miracles are of great importance, an importance which is rather odd, as surely creation is marvellous enough in itself, without any frills: and so I reverently tucked the spray in my bag and held my peace.

As soon as the precincts were left behind, the taximan treated me to his views on the holy life. 'This business of being a saint,' he remarked, 'really, there's nothing in it. Easy as falling off a log. For normal folk, that is to say. Of course, if one were given to porquerías (swinishness) it would be a different matter. But for the rest of us, no problem at all.'

Similar thoughts had been expressed to me by colleagues of his before.

'Then think how lucky these people are,' he continued. 'What a comfort to live in peace, without worry or occupation, all found and no taxes to pay!'

I asked how much he paid in taxes himself, for he had uttered the word with peculiar venom; and he replied, about three hundred and fifty pesetas (a little over two pounds) a quarter. It was iniquitous for a married man, yet men were expected to marry. And he would have liked to raise plenty of children but, with the fiscal authorities bleeding him white, he had to content himself with four. Next we moved on to politics, a field in which his ideas again were simple and definite. 'Whatever happens, it will all be one,' he asserted. 'The monarchy now, that everyone keeps on about . . . Whether they restore it, whether they don't, will make no difference to me. Pues, it's not worth thinking over.'

We drove first through forest, up a steep and winding road striped zebra-fashion where the sun broke through the trees, with an occasional glimpse of the cold and brilliant peaks of Gredos on the right. Then having reached the summit we ran easily down to the gentle slopes of La Vera and the valley beyond, richly planted with tobacco, figs, oranges, lemons and Indian corn. Here men were playing

137

cards in the open air outside the village cafés, while women and boys rested from work in the fields on the grassy banks along the way. The warmth and life of the scene brought a sense of joy and well-being after the deadening cold of the Sierra: it was like flying from wintry London to sunny flowery Nice, yet only a mountain range had divided the two.

Now Paco the driver discovered a fresh grievance, in that the road, smooth as a ribbon to the boundary of Avila province, became abruptly awful as we crossed into that of Caceres. 'This carretera, so-called, is used by lorries, buses and motorcoaches from Madrid,' he grimly pointed out. 'What are they going to say about it once they get home? We shall be the laughing-stock of the capital.' The prospect worried him a great deal more than the pummelling we ourselves received as the car jolted along over the mounds and through the gullies.

Plentiful mountain streams rushed down the slope and under stone bridges so decrepit that trees had burst their walls and thrust their branches through them. For all the driver had said, there was hardly a vehicle to be seen, only the immemorial procession of bronzed and wrinkled peasants on horse or mule, water jars or saddlebags slung behind them. A crowd of young people came by on foot, singing lustily and banging on various instruments: a marriage, Paco said, and a good one too. If it were a wedding of common people it would have to be early, at nine o'clock, but when people can afford to pay it may be celebrated at any hour. And afterwards they would keep it up for days, three perhaps or four, presumably until the money ran out, for Spaniards never tire of pleasure.

Presently we came to Jarandilla, where I had hoped to visit the castle in which the Emperor Carlos V had stayed until Yuste was ready; but Turismo had got there first and turned it into a parador. Castles, palaces, monasteries, patrician country houses, nothing is spared. Since I knew all too well how things would be inside, we did not stop but drove straight on to Yuste, the Jeronomite monastery where the Emperor, tired of power, glory and intrigue, ended his days, riding, gardening, reading, experimenting, playing with little don Juan, the future hero of Lepanto, and devoutly praying.

It is a fine stone cluster in a spacious garden, with tall plane and eucalyptus trees, oranges and lemons, a trout pond and a wood, standing halfway up the mountain. A spreading walnut waved its boughs in the courtyard, just as in the Emperor's own day. Everything spoke of peace, order and tranquillity now, although when the mighty Charles, master of Europe, lived there, he was quite unable to prevent the villagers driving off his cows, poaching his trout and hurling stones at don Juan. But no grandee of Spain ever was or ever will be a hero to the people round about.

An amiable monk, fat and smiling, came forward to bid us welcome and conduct us to the chapel – 'us', for Paco was determined to miss nothing – where the Emperor's corpse had lain in a niche below the High Altar, mass being said above it, as directed in his will. He had taken the usual keen interest of Spanish kings in his approaching demise and burial, even to the point of attending a dress rehearsal, as it were, of his own requiem; but the persistent legend of his being carried alive through the grounds in his coffin was dismissed by the monk as bosh.

'The Emperor was a man of sense,' he declared, speaking as one who knew him well.

Having shown us what little of the monastery the public is allowed to see, he passed us on to a lay custodian for a tour of the imperial apartments. All was bare, severe and dismal, in keeping with the Emperor's gloomy cast of mind. There were rooms hung all in black, in mourning for his mad mother Joan, austere offices, a sombre dining-hall and bedchamber, kept as they always were without a single pleasant or relieving touch. Adjoining the imperial bedroom was the privy in which Philip II, after his father's death, spent an uncomfortable two nights, his filial piety and respect forbidding him to occupy the room itself. It was like him to make the gesture once the man was safely dead: previously he had a spy installed, watching the Emperor's every move in case there was any sign of his wishing to repossess the power. Nearby was another narrow den where the bodyguards had slept, their helmets still hanging on the wall, Austrians, the only troops that Charles fully trusted. These gave an amusing word to the language, incidentally: heavily whiskered and forever shouting 'bei Gott!', they came to be known as the *bigotes*, which has been the Castilian for moustaches ever since. They and the gentlemen in waiting had but a dreary time of it after the pomp and circumstance of days gone by; and the ennui and impatience they expressed in their letters home are in notable contrast to the unctuous commentaries of the monks, delighted to harbour so devout and illustrious a guest. He was anything but a profitable one, however, for he never paid them a penny. After he was gone they looked to his heir for alms; but Philip coldly replied, 'You couldn't have kept my father a year without feathering your nest.' As an example of how the rich stay rich, the pair of them could hardly be bettered.

The *custode* drew our attention to the stool on which the Emperor rested his leg in his frequent, agonizing attacks of gout. 'A martyr he was, a martyr, poor holy man,' he observed, discreetly passing over the fact that his martyrdom was mainly self-induced. He was a rare trencherman, gross yet finicky: rich meats were procured from far and wide, and there was no end of to-do if they were lost or spoiled on the journey. Well knowing the torments that would follow, he still refused himself nothing, and in the constant struggle between prudence and appetite, prudence was always defeated.

Yuste was burned and sacked in 1809 by the French, who went through the land like the plagues of Egypt; and in 1821 the Liberals finished the job, carrying off what little was left and stabling their horses in the church, in the fine old liberal tradition. Thus a great deal of what we saw was reconstituted, yet nothing was lost thereby. The spirit of the Emperor hung over the place as if he had but recently died, both in the rooms and in the garden, where the *custode* presently gave us leave to wander at will. And there was a poignancy about it all, the great man ending his days in this smiling region he loved, content to leave Spain's future in other hands, sure of her greatness, unconscious that her downward path was already preparing. Here is eternal spring, he remarked as he lay dying, and this was the feeling the valley gave, fresh and green in the depths of winter and suffused in warm yellow light.

Within the monastery a bell was calling the monks to office, as has been said continually here for over five and a half centuries. The sound followed us down the hill, gentle yet assured, until we swung into the winding road back to Arenas and it was lost in cheerful secular noise. Now we ran across one wedding party after another, the whole district seemingly convulsed by matrimony. The lull between the solemnity of Advent and the penitential rigours of Lent is a favourite marrying time in Spain, just as English couples speed to the altar before the ending of the financial year. Old and young, women and men, all were in tearing high spirits, banging drums or blowing whistles, some mounted, others on foot, while the wineskins passed from hand to hand and jokes flew fast and furious.

One festive crew spread out across the road, obliging Paco to stop, and carried us off to a tavern, there to drink wine and eat slices of *lomo*, loin of pork, deliciously cured. They were on their way from the church to the bride's parental roof, under which, according to custom, her mother sat waiting alone: for such is the grief of losing a daughter, in theory, that no mother can bear to attend her marriage. Nevertheless, they seemed in no particular hurry to console the afflicted woman or to arrive for the wedding feast she was to offer. It was clear, both from the fact of their roping us strangers in and from a certain hilarity in themselves, that they had paused a good few times by the way already; and now, as cup followed cup, they grew more and more disposed to settle down, while constantly reminding each other that it was really time to be off. The bride's grandfather favoured the party with a song of his

own composition, which was received with acclaim: someone followed with anecdotes of the groom in his boyhood,
largely concerned with the losing and finding of goats. The
happy pair, both sturdy red-cheeked peasants, spoke not at
all but steadily ate and drank, with an occasional burst of
wild giggles. At last we got away, though not without some
argument, and left them going strong, howling for more
wine and more *lomo*, and demanding that the landlord show
himself, to receive their felicitations. I hoped that whatever
dainties the bride's mother had prepared for them were of a
kind that did not spoil.

As we got into the car again, there was a mighty burst of
guffaws from the tavern and Paco gravely shook his head.

'Falta de educación,' he remarked, dismissing the revellers with a lordly wave of the hand.

The word and the gesture reinforced an impression that I
first had got as together we paced the imperial garden
walks. For some mysterious reason, Paco's personality had
changed, expanded, blossomed out. On the way to Yuste,
such views as he expressed had been entirely predictable:
just as monks were primarily tax-evaders and sponges, so
royalty was chiefly concerned with keeping a foot on the
necks of honest men. Once there, he began the tour with
the mulish looks of a Spaniard who is not to be impressed
or taken in by anything whatsoever. But by the time we
reached the grounds all these had gone, his manner
became infinitely gracious and he bore himself, tub as he
was, with an air of notable consequence; and in the
tavern he was amiable and aloof, pleased to observe the
junketings of *hoi polloi* but refusing to sink to their level.

'No idea of what is seemly,' he added now, lofty as
ever.

'But such hospitality!' I said. 'Princely! The Emperor
himself could not have done more.'

Indeed, he would not have done half as much.

'They meant well,' Paco conceded. 'But it was not for
them to drag the Señora into their family doings. And the
place was not as befitted. If the Señora permits, I shall

142

offer her some refreshment in a sitio I know of, further on, that in every way is more suitable.'

This was said so regally that I saw at last what was up. In a wonderfully Spanish way, Paco was 'identifying' with Carlos V. The hostility he had shown at the start was purely mechanical, his response to an abstract idea: brought to life, embodied, clothed, imperially housed, the Emperor was quite another kettle of fish, and Paco had taken him over.

The dream possessed him for the rest of the journey home. At times I felt almost uncomfortable to think that he should be driving me, and not the other way round. There were no more complaints of the *carretera*, since now it was his. The *sitio* he brought me to was the pleasantest touch of all, for it resembled the wedding tavern in every particular, except that *lomo* was not to be had, nothing but sausage and cheese.

At the doors of the hostel, however, he came down to earth in a hurry, gave me my bill – with the refreshments discreetly added on – inquired what my future wishes might be and promised to give them his best attention.

'Always at your service, Señora,' he said, clearing his throat in horrendous fashion; and drove away.

15

Next morning, as arranged, he appeared on the stroke of nine, all set for Guadalupe. To the local way of thinking, this was the crack of dawn: unused to such early hours, the hostel had lent me an alarm clock – which fiercely ticked the night away but failed to ring – and bidden me find my breakfast *en la calle*, to which I gladly agreed. It was therefore a pleasant surprise to see the taxi bowling up so punctually on the minute; but I realized at once, as it stopped, that this was a special and solemn occasion. Yellow with dust the evening before, it now shone and sparkled as if new from the factory: a bunch of pink paper roses adorned the image of St. Christopher; and Paco himself, the homely blue overalls discarded, was resplendent in navy serge, with a white peaked cap of maritime aspect at a jaunty angle on his head.

All this was in honour of the Virgin of Guadalupe, whose shrine is the second holiest in Spain and the very heart and core of *Hispanidad*. Paco was true Spanish working-class in his deep devotion to the Mother of God and total cynicism in religious affairs generally. For many years, he now revealed, he had longed to visit her in this most sumptuous of her homes, but never got the chance.

'And who knows, I might never have, if you hadn't happened by,' he pointed out, clearly impressed by the workings of Fate. 'That's the best of foreigners – always on the move.'

144

He spoke as if Guadalupe were at the other end of the world, instead of a bare sixty miles from his door; but he plainly meant what he said, and regarded my coming as providential.

We stopped for my cup of coffee and soon were on our way. Once clear of the town Paco removed his cap and placed it carefully in a box until he should need it for the ceremonial entry into Guadalupe. We were making a small detour first, to look at the Cuevas de el Aguila, eleven kilometres from Arenas and said to be among the finest known. And certainly they were magnificent, a veritable fairy playground, with fantastic stalagmites and stalactites resembling the pipes of an organ, the folds of some huge garment or a feathery angel's wing; and as we wandered through the dim echoing vaults we came on all manner of curiously lifelike figures, a rhinoceros, a boar, a bull, a crocodile, as well as the Virgen del Pilar, del Carmen, de Guadalupe, a St Joseph with the Child, friars and monks, a Buddha. It was hard to believe that they had not been sculpted, but had simply come about through the dripping water. Here and there cliffs rose steeply, sparkling white or saffron, orange, pink and red, while shallow pools threw lovely trembling patterns on the rocks above and deeper ones lay calm and black and still, as if there could be no fathoming them.

The whole place was beautifully lit; but, with the wonted excess of zeal, the management had decided to cheer things up with a steady blare of piped music. We were subjected now to the Tales from the Vienna Woods, now to the Gold and Silver waltz, turn and turn about, until our brains reeled – or mine at least, for Paco was charmed with the horrid shindy and described it as 'precioso'.

The caves were discovered some years ago by a mischievous boy. He was trespassing on private land, busy with a catapult, when he noticed the mouth of a tunnel and informed the proprietor. This gentleman investigated and found the grotto, an obvious gold-mine; and when it was ready for public showing, he took on the boy's elder brothers as guides, himself collecting the fees. But there now arose a fine point of equity. As the boy's family saw it, they were entitled to a share of the takings as well: the owner denied this, saying the boy had no business to poach his *finca* and therefore had improperly found the caves. As neither party would yield, a lawsuit pended, and the chances are, is pending still; but meanwhile things went on very comfortably, the brothers guiding in smart uniforms, doing well out of tips and freely canvassing public opinion in their favour.

We resumed our journey, passing by Oropesa, whose fourteenth century castle, needless to say, is now a parador. It was an early one, however, early enough to receive a visit from Somerset Maugham and his suite: the writer's somewhat flowery comments, inscribed on vellum, hang in many a tourist office. Here we stopped at a garage for petrol and a snack, expecting the usual weary *bocadilla* and greatly cheered to find *carabineros*, fat, rosy and fresh as if straight from the sea.

Up to now the country was flat and rather dull, but once Oropesa was left behind we soon caught sight of the Guadalupe mountains. The characteristic features of Estremadura began to appear, the evergreen oaks with lively black pigs around them, the terraced gardens of fruit and vegetables, the rustling streams, the peasants with faces scorched so dark in summer it lasts the winter through, the weird rock formations, the flaming gashes in the mountainside. Here too were the lovely groves of olive, stretching away as far as the eye could see: men were at the harvest, whipping the feathery branches with long supple wands that made a wham wham wham like the sound of washerwomen slapping clothes on a rock, while girls gathered up the berries and pigs rooted joyously in the grass beside them: herds of cattle and flocks of goat, driven by small children, streamed past with a soft jangling of their bells.

Glossy cars full of elegant people were travelling the same road as ourselves. One expensive monster that overtook us had the marking CH, to the great delight of Paco, who informed me that this meant Chile. 'From all over Spanish

America they pour in, to visit Guadalupe,' he told me grandly, 'bringing their private coaches, regardless of expense.' I had some idea that CH stood for Confédération Helvétique, and the occupants of the car indeed had Switzerland written all over them, but Paco was happy in his *ilusión* and not for anything would I have disturbed it.

He continued holding forth on the theme of La Madre España and her respectful children overseas for some little while. From his manner of speaking, one might have supposed that we were still in the age of the *conquistadores*. And so, as far as he was concerned, we probably were. Spaniards have none of the easy English forward-looking that simply closes the account with things gone by: their past is always alive in them, and very much part of their present. The formidable Spanish pride is not inherent or racial, but springs from a notion that they are still, somehow, rulers of the world. Outsiders may find this engagingly absurd, but the Spaniard either heeds them not or discourages levity by wrapping his imperial grandeur yet more firmly round him.

There was no occasion for Paco to do this, as I cheerfully agreed to all he said, however preposterous. And by now we were running through the mountains up to the tableland where Guadalupe perches on high, commanding glorious views in every direction. At the very edge of the *pueblo* itself we paused, while Paco resumed his cap of office, then mounted the narrow winding cobbled street that led to the monastery. Here we parted company, I to look for rooms in the Hospedería Monasterio, he to mingle with the pilgrim hordes surging about the holy places; and, although we never met again, for the rest of the day I frequently glimpsed his round white cap among them, clear for a moment, then swallowed up, like the moon travelling through clouds.

The Hospedería was full to bursting, as I should have foreseen, but they gave me a billet in the annex, suitably called the *habitaciones góticas*. A friar, or lay brother, led the way through long dismal stone passages to a room of penitential aspect, whose temperature stood roughly at zero. No doubt accustomed to mortification, he seemed amazed when I ventured to bring this fact to his notice; but with a kindly 'no se preocupa' he hurried away, returning with a heater that hissed and roared as if on the point of explosion.

'That should warm you a little,' he smiled, 'but be careful not to touch it.'

The warning was unnecessary, for I never beheld a more wicked and frightening stove; and, chilled as I was, it came almost as a relief when, after five minutes, the friar burst in again, regretted that it was wanted elsewhere and carried it off. Now I gingerly prodded the bed, finding the springs sound, the mattress firm and new, and the pillows plump: the linen was snowy white, but so damp that moisture might have been wrung from it in heavy drops. No one dreams of airing bedclothes in Spain, where indeed for most of the year the climate makes it superfluous but where, when it is needed at all, it is needed badly. Marvelling as ever at the fortitude of the race, and not without misgivings on my own account, I unpacked and tidied up as well as numb fingers allowed and went across the street for a reviving lunch at the parador.

The limousines that had shot past us on the way were now drawn up in rows outside it, as in a royal enclosure; and the restaurant was packed with lunchers all with the unmistakable New World gloss. The fingers of men and women alike sparkled with jewels, and on every side the soft trailing Mexican brogue was heard. I am familiar with the various Mexican types through watching gringo westerns, where the roles assigned them are either villainous or despicable, except for the odd lovely senõrita who charms the Yanqui hero until he bethinks him of the girl at home and rides off into the sunset with a brave little song on his lips: thus, there was a certain piquency in spotting them all here, as it were in translation, dressed up to the nines and giving commands to the waiters in the lordliest fashion, as if they owned the place. And up to a point they had reason, the monastery having been vastly enriched by the returning conquerors of Mexico, among them Cortez, who settled a handsome share of all the plunder on the Virgin in the hope she would put in a word for him on Judgement Day.

No doubt she will gladly do so, if all that is said of her be true. She it was, Spaniards maintain, who led the *conquistadores* to victory all over the New World, and followed with motherly interest that coaxing of Indians into the Church which was, of course, their primary aim. And in our own sadly reduced times, she has not lost touch with public affairs. Back in the Hospedería that afternoon, I came on an old copy of the *Revista Mariana*, announcing her recent appointment as mayor of Medina de las Torres, with a charming account of the ceremony and of the grace with which she took her baton of office, all described exactly as if she had been a living woman: one half expected to read of her accepting a bouquet from some little child, with a smile and a few kindly words.

In that same periodical was also the story of one of her many miracles. In 1519 a Juan Velez of Pontejos, Santander, had been taken up with several others, sentenced to death and clapped in chains at Laredo. He helped his companions strike their fetters off, but could do nothing with his own: the comrades ran away and left him; and when darkness fell he jumped from the window of his prison to the rocky ground some fifty feet below, crawling painfully out of the town as best he might. Once more he strove to knock the chains from his legs, but without success. Then he prayed with all his heart that the 'most blessed Lady and glorious Virgin Maria de Guadalupe' would come to his aid. The chains at once dropped off, first from the right leg, then from the left; and he came to Guadalupe to give thanks for the mercy received from her blessed Son through her intercession. And this too was related with a matter-of-fact simplicity, far removed from the beflowered style of most hagiographers and much like that of a newspaperman who had covered the events himself.

Apart from its Gothic Rooms, which may not have been intended for winter use, the Hospedería was wholly delightful. It was full of pilgrims, priest, friar and nun, parties of students and *beatas*, those devout old ladies who are in and out of church all day; and yet the atmosphere could only be described as jolly. No lists of rules or pious exhortations hung upon the walls, a bar was provided and freely used, and jugs of excellent wine were brought with every meal as a matter of course; and still one never lost the feeling of a religious house, with all its peculiar grace and comfort.

It was, of course, too much to hope that there would be no tele. After dinner we assembled in the parlour to watch, until it was time for the New Year's midnight Mass. There was a recital of lovely songs from every part of Spain, that folk-music so rich and varied and so seldom heard: nor indeed was it really heard now, as the company prattled blithely all the way through. It was followed by a play of crime and detection, *estilo americano*, but whose Spanish author had somehow failed to grasp the exigencies of the *genre*: clues were plentiful but not germane, suspects were fiercely harangued before disappearing for ever, while the criminal figured not at all until the very moment of his arrest. In contrast to the music, however, this shocking nonsense was followed with strained attention, one portly Franciscan, a veritable Friar Tuck, puffing excitedly at his cigar and roaring with laughter every other minute. I am sure there is no reason why Franciscans should not smoke, but so many of them are at it nowadays that the cigar has almost become an adjunct, like the sandals, habit and knotted rope.

Towards midnight we moved as one to the basilica, there to mingle with the Mexican brigade in all its splendour. The church, beautiful in itself, was beautifully kept, the altars banked with fresh flowers and hosts of candles burning in honour of the day. High above the chief altar was the Virgin's throne, where she stood holding the baby, both in gorgeous robes, their dark faces surmounted by top-heavy crowns: like the Morena of Monserrat, the Madonna of Guadalupe is dusky, and both are said to have been carved by the Evangelist Luke. The parocco and his acolytes were spick and span, the mass was sung with decorum and precision, no one scratched himself or got mixed up, and the entire proceedings were most unSpanish. The one fanciful touch came from the music, with the creed in a Mozartian setting like a chorus from *Don Giovanni* and somebody warbling *flamenco* all through Holy Communion. Such things are probably left to the personal caprice of the choir master: in my day I have knelt at Spanish altar-rails to every conceivable tune, from Schubert's 'Serenade' to the 'Song of the Volga Boatmen'; and no one ever appears to think it strange.

As in Avila, all the while that mass went on we could hear the youth of the *pueblo* marching round and round, drumming, yelling and pumping away at the *zambomba*: it was like being in a fort beleaguered by savage tribes. Then came the *Ite, missa est*, followed by the usual graceless rush for the doors, leaving the celebrant to tidy up on his own. Spaniards may be the world's best Catholics, as they believe, but their manners in church are wholly deplorable. To avoid the buffeting and jostling, I went to see the crib, a remarkable specimen and even richer than that of Santo Tomás. A lamb was twice as large as a camel, and the Kings were half as tall again as the orange trees; and, to lend the whole a *típico* air, there was added a windmill, a family of pigs and a countryman playing the guitar, as well as geese and swans cheek by jowl with elephants and Jews under the coconut palms, all with that sublime indifference to scale.

But now a sacristan was turning off the lights and old women in carpet slippers shuffled round the votive stands, blowing out the candles and collecting the butts together. As I left the church, there was an elderly man in shabby clothes at the top of the stairway down to the plaza, hands clasped behind his back, hair silvery in the moonlight, gazing upon the turbulent crowd below. Something in the stance, with the leonine head cocked to one side, was very familiar, and so, as I passed him, was the firm distinguished profile: there had been a time when I knew this person well,

151

and yet I had walked all the way home before I realized, with stupefaction, who it was. My failure to recognize him must have been due to his being the last man alive I would have expected to see in Spain; for, long years ago in Paris, he was the most intransigent of exiles, with a bitter loathing of Franco and all his works. It would have been scarcely more of a shock to find Casals and Picasso strolling together along the Alcalá.

I turned and hurried back to the *plaza*. He was still there, still alone, lost in contemplation, his features, once so mobile, set and blank as a mask. I remembered them ablaze with anger, scorn, despair or lit with ferocious mockery, all too often directed against myself. We were the closest of friendly enemies. His comminations seemed to ring in my ears now as I stood and watched him. How could I endure that vile country, how breathe its air without choking, did I not realize that visits by foreigners were taken to mean their approval, was I at heart a fascist . . .

We could hardly take things up again from just the point where we left them. And there was nothing really to say, or, rather, that needed saying. 'I am old, and politics have lost all sense for me. I only want my country, my people, my language, our food and our weather, for the last few years that remain.'

And so I went away without a word and left him, the implacable anti-Catholic and anti-imperialist, standing before the greatest of Spanish shrines to the glory of the Church and of military conquest, to think his thoughts in peace.

In the morning I joined a group to visit the treasures of the community. The priest who led us was jovial and down to earth, with the assurance of a man seldom, if ever, contradicted. He marshalled us hot foot through the chapels, with their glories of painting and sculpture, but lingered in love over the Virgin's regalia, boasting of it freely and, peasant-like, mainly in terms of money. As he quoted the price of a single diamond in the prodigious crown offered by the nation in 1928 his speech grew blurred, as if his mouth were watering; and when we came to the 'rico' mantle, said to be the richest in the world, presented by the community in the sixteenth century, his eyes shone and he rubbed his hands for glee.

'Half a million pearls!' he chortled. 'And all matching!'

Here the excellent man had allowed himself to be carried away, for the pearls in fact number a mere hundred and fifty thousand; but there are a hundred and eighty diamonds as well, all of prime quality, bearing witness to the Order's wealth in days gone by. A jingle of the period runs:

> Quien es conde y desea ser duque,
> Metese fraile en Guadalupe.

(He who is Count and would be Duke, Let him turn monk at Guadalup'.) And apart from the crown and the various gorgeous robes, there was a grand array of brooches, rings and bracelets, studded with diamonds, rubies and emeralds, all offerings from the pious rich.

To us it may seem childish, frivolous and alien to the humble simplicity of Christ's mother, but I have never known a Spaniard, however ascetic and devout himself, to take that view. Precious stones appear to have a spiritual value or meaning, intrinsic to them, unrelated to the sacrifice of the donor or the symbolism of the gift. No one could say of St Teresa that she cared a button for the things of this world, yet once when she was troubled in her mind she had a comforting vision of Our Lady who said that as proof of divine support she would give her a jewel: 'She then seemed to throw around my neck a most splendid necklace of gold, from which hung a cross of great value. The stones and gold were so different from any in this world, that there is nothing wherewith to compare them. The beauty of them is such as can be conceived by no imagination . . .' And in all the shrines of the country the faithful, priests, friars, nuns, laymen, are to be found contemplating these baubles with an almost devotional reverence. It is an odd trait in so austere a people, and conceivably had its root in the Jewish tradition, lingering on despite the efforts of the Holy Office.

The sight of all these treasures stimulated an old woman, herself lavishly bejewelled, into such a flood of reminiscence concerning the similar marvels she had seen elsewhere that the father bade her, for pity's sake, hold her peace and let him do the talking. She paused a moment and then swept on, becoming both the joke and the bore of the party, while he stood glumly by in frustration; but his turn was to come. The tour reached its climax at the stand, or *trono*, of the Virgin above the high altar, a number of historical scenes being painted on the back now turned towards us. The father at once pointed out one of these to his garrulous tormentor.

'Lepanto!' he said. 'Now, Señora, tell us all that happened at Lepanto.'

The lady pondered awhile, and gave it up. 'History was never my strong point,' she confessed, amid delighted mirth; and thereafter was dumb.

When we had duly admired the pictures, the priest, with a dramatic gesture, swung the shrine round on its revolving base and there stood the exquisite Morenita herself, whom previously we had but glimpsed from far below. We heard the story of her travels, from Byzantium to Rome, where Pope Gregory the Great had her carried in procession to help fight the plague that ravaged the city, then to Seville as the gift of the Pope to Archbishop San Leandro as a reward for his battles against Arianism, then to Guadalupe, where she was buried by clergy before the Arab invasions of the eighth century and where she was found again, miraculously preserved after five centuries of Arab occupation, by a shepherd in 1330. What with the finding of statues and the seeing of visions, be it said in passing, the services of shepherds, cowherds and goatherds to the Church in Spain have been well nigh incalculable.

After that, we respectfully kissed the hem of the Virgin's robe in turn. The discomfited lady outdid us all, with her curtseys and salutations and her air of one who knew *buenas costumbres*, even if vague about Lepanto. Then the priest accepted our offerings, fired a parting jest at the newly married couple and ogled the bride in a far from pastoral spirit before going his way.

I followed him out and asked if it would be possible for me to use the library.

'That is not for me to say,' he answered, staring. 'But why should you want to?'

To Spaniards, the thought of anyone actually reading often comes as a surprise. I told him I wanted to fish about in the archives.

'That – no!' he said, with decision.

He proved to be right, and my subsequent efforts to gain access to them came to nothing. The key was mislaid, the archivist was ill, I should never find what I was looking for, the room was too cold to work in, and other such well-worn excuses. As a rule they collapse at the sweet chink of coin, but not here. It was disappointing, because the place must be a veritable treasure-house of Spanish *Americana*. One of the illustrations to the *Guia de Guadalupe*, by Fr Arturo Alvarez, was an excerpt from the baptismal certificate of the first Indian converts in 1496; and I would greatly have relished a full account of this gratifying spread of the Gospel, blow by blow.

In that same Guide I read that the star of the monastery had begun to fade at the end of the eighteenth century, when the grandeur of Spain was in eclipse and devotion to the Virgen del Pilar, at Zaragoza, was becoming nation-wide: Spanish authors have a curious way of writing about the Virgins of here and there as if they were all quite separate and unconnected people.

I spent a few more days in this delightful place, enjoying the Zurbarán and other masterpieces at my leisure and wandering through the magnificent country around. The New Year influx streamed away, and instead of motor horns and the racket of scooters there was the quiet clip-clop of horses' hooves and the homely rumble of wooden wheels. I moved from the Gothic Chambers to a warm room with a view, and fell more in love with the Hospedería than ever. The *pueblo* itself had infinite charm with its narrow winding streets, the upper storeys of the little houses jutting out and supported by pillars, with geraniums still in flower tumbling from the window-boxes. Everything here spoke of the old order, with its peace and dignity and calm. The one up-to-date building was the fine new railway station, with trim white and green buildings, complete in every detail down to a bar and a newspaper kiosk. All that it lacked was the railway line, for which the town had been hopefully waiting some years. Paciencia! It may come yet, adding a new miracle to the Virgin's already extensive list. Meanwhile, when the time came to leave, there was the old familiar rickety coach, everything about it just as always, except that I had an eight-year-old boy on my knee for most of the journey.

The next two days were given up to answering letters. While in Madrid, I had these sent in care of a friend rather than expose them to the hazards of the residencia or of the poste restante; and when I set off for the country, she had undertaken to forward them to various points along my route. Inquiries, however, produced the invariable reply 'No, nothing for the Señora', which I heard with the usual mixture of relief and disappointment, together with great surprise. Now all was explained. My friend, on thinking it over, had decided against the arrangement. I was supposed to be enjoying myself, and correspondence would only molest me. To the Spanish mind, letters are merely pieces of paper covered with words: they have little bearing on real life and hence no claim to serious attention. So there they all were, in a dreadful mound on her escritoire; and, having sent off urgent cables in every direction, I applied myself to working slowly through it.

When I could emerge again, it was to find the capital more than ever thronged with festive crowds. Christmas and the New Year were over, and now they were boiling up with fresh vigour for the Three Kings. All down the Paseo de Prado, loudspeakers were bawling songs, in which the sentries on guard at government buildings lustily joined. Everyone seemed fairly bursting with gaiety and excitement, and the hubbub was indescribable.

In the afternoon I set off for Valladolid by the TALGO.

All the other travellers were Spanish and all partook of the gargantuan lunch, so that the long caterpillar of a coach presently reeked of fish, steak, oranges and coffee; and after that, they all fell asleep, their snores vying with and at times surmounting the canned music from which, even here, there apparently was to be no relief.

It was a beautiful day and a beautiful journey. Once the mountains were left behind, the vast undulating plain spread out in a golden haze, with here and there a poplar wood, a luminous waterway fringed with willow, or the bell-tower of a church, clear and sharp against the sky. At Valladolid, the sun was going down and the cold was bitter. This did not deter the people from bringing their children out to admire the tinsel finery in honour of the Kings, for no extreme of cold or heat deters a Spaniard from doing what he wants, although a few drops of rain will have him off the street in a flash. The main thoroughfares seethed with country folk up for the fiesta, shoving and heaving and blundering into each other like so many cattle; and the amplifiers nesting in the *faroles* out-bawled even those of Madrid, producing such a clamour there was no telling what the tune was supposed to be.

Away from these, with their shops, cafés and garish neon-lighting, all was quiet, dim and deserted. In the shadowy old quarters stood, like prehistoric monsters, the ungainly instruments of demolition, halted by the fiesta, biding their time until the whistles blew and set them to work again, clawing down and munching up the past, clearing room for more and still more unsightly concrete boxes: a process which, I later found, was a source of tremendous pride and satisfaction to the citizens.

For a couple of hours I patrolled the streets and then, frozen through, returned to my hotel, hot and airless as a sauna bath. It cheered me greatly, and so did the evening meal when at last it got on the table, the cooks having all slipped out to see the fun and the waiters too.

A posse, headed by the manager, sallied forth to round them up, while I settled down with the newspapers. One of

158

these had a story which clearly it thought most edifying and which, in the right hands, could have made a splendidly wicked film. A little boy had written from his pueblo in Valencia to the Three Kings, without further address, asking for books and toys. The post office sent the letter to Seville, where the Ateneo, or Athenaeum, always makes a tremendous splash at the Epiphany. Fired by the boy's simple trust, and possibly by the chance of brightening the Falange 'image' as well, the Ateneo cajoled Sevillan stores into providing the goods and appointed a committee to convey them to Valencia. Their presentation was made in the presence of all the village authorities, to the strains of the village band, thus lending it 'caracteres de solemnidad'; and better still, the President of the Consejo de Economía Nacional came all the way from Barcelona to pronounce a few words of affectionate and pious exhortation to the little boy and of greeting to the villagers, assembled to witness the charming act. The child expressed his thanks 'con visible emoción'; and may well think twice before approaching the Kings again.

The next morning broke harder than ever, now with an opaque fog and leaden sky. At ten o'clock the streets were empty but for the dauntless devout old women making their way to Mass. In the Museo Nacional de Escultura, there was not a soul but the men in charge, muffled up to the ears and torpid from the cold. I was visiting it because a friend of mine in Madrid had been so gravely shocked to hear that I never had, and said so much on the matter that I dared not face him again with the omission unrepaired. It was only afterwards that I learned he had never been in it himself.

But I had often admired the building, one of the finest in Valladolid, with a particularly splendid façade. The architect never saw it, for, having fully worked out all the plans, he killed himself, in 1490. The sculptures were mostly *policromades*, the painted carvings in which Spaniards delight, although to a less exuberant taste there is something a little doll-like in the rosy flesh and coloured draperies of the living subjects, while the dead often appear to have been 'fixed' by an American mortician. Apart from the show-pieces of the masters, Berruguete, Juan de Juni, Fernandez, there are some enchanting anonymous pieces, among them a Mary Magdalene in the Desert, eighteenth century, reposing under a palm tree in her flowered dress, gazing piously upward, one elbow supported by a skull. Another Magdalene, by Pedro de Mena, with her straw dress, long hair and thin harassed features, made a curiously modern, not to say hippie, impression, although her date was 1664.

Every single piece had a religious subject, natural enough at a time when the Church was patron in chief, yet homely secular touches had crept in here and there. At the Lord's Supper by Adrian Alvarez and Pedro de Torres they served a roasted sucking-pig, a delicacy that seems never far from the Castilian mind, for I have met it in equally improbable surroundings at Burgos and elsewhere; and in the choir-stalls of San Benito el Real, on a panel depicting the marriage at Cana, the most life-like figure is of a dog devouring a bone. And there was a certain impish realism about the Duke and Duchess of Lerma kneeling in prayer, her Grace apparently asking, 'Must we really do this?' and the Duke replying, 'The lower classes expect it.' But the effect as a whole is of deadening orthodoxy, a vast array of Virgins, Holy Families, Crucifixions, Burials, Saints, Early Fathers and Miracles, many superb in themselves but wanting their rightful place in cathedral or church to make an impact, the very abundance of the collection defeating its purpose.

And then there was the bitter cold. In summer, one is hot and cross, in winter, freezing and cross: neither makes for the appreciation of art. Today there was no heating what-ever in this huge edifice, such amenity being reserved for Sundays. The unhappy *custodes* marched vigorously up and down, their heavy tread and squeaking boots a further bar to concentration. Many rooms were so dark that one could barely see across them. Sometimes an attendant would turn on a light, mostly he would declare that the current had failed and that anyhow the works were 'deficiente' and I should not like them. They plainly looked on me as an intruder, and thought I had no business to be there.

One of them, more friendly, volunteered to show me something worth the rest of the pieces put together. Blowing on his fingers, he led the way through a marvellous patio to a chapel with a number of eighteenth-century statues of no special charm and a full-size figure of Death. This was the promised treat, and he indicated the worms writhing in and out of the ribs as proudly as if he himself were the artist.

'Wouldn't you swear they were real?' he demanded. 'Hombre! look at the fellow there. Doesn't he seem to move? That's my idea of a statue, lively and to the point. You get tired of the other stuff. I often slip out, when we're not too busy, for a quiet smoke in here with the old amigo looking on.'

He did not fail, as we retraced our steps, to remark that all of us would resemble the old *amigo* in time and, what was more, none could foretell how soon it would be.

I was glad to escape from this worthy man and his enlivening comments to the warmth and bustle of the café San Pablo across the way. It was full of stout little Army officers in ceremonial kit, with brocade belts, mauve sashes and swords, gulping a hot drink before they paraded outside the Capitania in honour of the Kings. There were family parties too, the children clasping the gifts brought them by the Kings – space ships, robots, revolvers, machine-guns, with here and there an electric guitar.

As soon as I had thawed, I went on to the house in which Miguel de Cervantes Saavedra lived from 1603 to 1604, for reasons which vary with the biographer. Some say he was following the Court, which Philip III had moved to Valladolid in a brief attempt to re-establish that city as the capital, and from which, as a wounded veteran of Lepanto, Cervantes might expect some preferment. Others declare he was defending a lawsuit which arose from his money troubles. Be this as it may, for a poverty-stricken man he was very pleasantly lodged, in a charming house with a small sunk garden and well-proportioned if narrow rooms.

Two guides, looking like jovial pirates, wrangled awhile as to which should take me round, the loser getting the job. There was his study, with a well-fingered first edition of *Don Quixote* on the table, a bedroom, dining-room and kitchen, all furnished in the simple, austere, appealing Spanish way, and a workroom for his daughter, with cushions spread on a dais in the more voluptuous Arab style, a spindle and various objects of devotion. Of his wife there was neither mention nor souvenir, and it seems he never spoke of her. As to how much, if any, of *Don Quixote* was written here, accounts vary again. Some allege it was the whole of Book One, a claim naturally upheld by those in charge of the house, while another school believes that the entire work was composed in gaol. Fidelity to the concept is of greater importance to Spanish minds than accuracy of detail, and we can take our choice; but, as the first edition appeared in 1605, it does seem likely that the book was pondered here at least, and that in these quiet bourgeois surroundings the greatest comic story of the world was partly conceived.

'I suppose you have read the novel,' the amiable guide remarked at the end of our tour. 'It's about a loco (madman), isn't it?'

'Yes, a man who lost his wits from too much reading.'

'That could very well happen,' the guide said, looking pleased. 'I never had time for any reading at all.'

He appeared to be congratulating himself on a narrow escape, while I was refreshed by his candour. His lack of interest too, so national and sublime, struck me as entirely appropriate and in keeping. If it comes to that, I have often wondered how familiar with *Don Quixote* a good many well-read persons at home really are. The association in their minds with windmills, for example, might be a pointer: that adventure was anything but his funniest, but it was his first, suggesting that, dismayed by the undoubted longueurs of the masterpiece, they read no further. And the English word 'quixotic' has taken on a meaning quite unrelated to the Knight's persona. In his way, he was as good a

Spaniard as Sancho Panza himself, wholly unconcerned with other people, no matter how distressed: he was a prime egomaniac, whose real lunacy showed not in his fantastic exploits but in the attempt to revive what was dead and gone, the typically Spanish effort to breathe life into corpses.

The Casa de Cervantes, like the Museo Nacional, had been exclusively mine. A refugee from the madding crowd in Spain is sure of sanctuary in a cultural institution. Outside, one could hardly move for the press of bodies, or think for the hurly-burly of public rejoicing. Children, riding their fathers' shoulders, beat one's head with balloons or anointed it with slavers of ice-cream, which despite the arctic weather most were licking. I fought my way to the Florida, an eating-house I recollected as one of monastic calm: as I passed the door, some one put a record on the player and lo! the Beatles burst out in full cry.

Afterwards I took a walk through the city, the processions now being over and the multitudes gradually thinning Valladolid is not immediately felt as a whole, as Segovia, Avila or Burgos are: it is sprawling and incoherent and the many beauties leap from their back-ground rather than blend with it. The Plaza Mayor was an exception, with its brick and stone façades, pink and silver, harmonious and trim; and the Campo Grande, lovely in summer, was pleasant enough today, the jasmine blooming, peacocks huddled under bushes, drowsy with cold, swans paddling up and down the mini-pond, and the plane-trees with their ochre leaves a vivid splash against the sullen sky.

But nowhere, not in Madrid itself, is there more repulsive new building. No doubt the mediaeval *barrios*, whose narrow crooked streets were rather more attractive to walk through than to live in, had to be cleared away; but one questions if the *viviendas* that replace them need have been quite so awful. Is it really beyond the power of man to design a block of flats which does not sicken all who behold it? And while these eyesores were hurriedly built, on the cheap, for urgent use, others as bad are the fruit of long and loving deliberation, proudly erect in all their horror as if glorying in their shame.

A notable instance is the Capucine church in the Plaza de España, a giant concrete hanger that could equally well be a cinema or a skating-rink. Evidently the fathers aimed to be 'with it', for, going inside, I found a sort of religious pop, to guitar accompaniment, wailing through amplifiers, whose mechanical deficiencies produced an occasional startling croak. This was the prelude to an evening mass; and, fair play for the Capuchinos, there was no nonsense about the mass itself. An immensely fat young priest, like Billy Bunter in Holy Orders, barked instructions over the microphone: Stand up! Kneel down! Say the responses! All together! Louder than that! Now be seated! Everyone smartly obeyed, up and down, up and down, like puppets worked by a string, apparently too engrossed in the drill to be alive to anything else: for when, in the course of the sermon, a small boy exploded a paper bag, a dirty look from Fr Bunter was the only reaction. As Communion was about to be given, he darted back to his microphone: Immodestly dressed women will not be allowed to receive! It all left me with a curious impression of having wandered into a reformatory, and the interior of the edifice living up to the exterior in every way, I was glad to see the last of it.

Next morning, long before it was light, a clamour of sirens and whistles announced that Valladolid was at work again. After breakfast I hired a car to go the the Monastery of San Rafael de la Santa Espina, some thirty miles away, as a relief from the march of progress. As we passed row upon dismal row of its manifestations, I felt that everywhere soon will be exactly like everywhere else, and we can all stay at home; but at the city edge these broke abruptly off, as if progress, like fever, were something to keep in confinement. Once beyond the military airport, where the fog was too thick to allow of flying – 'that never happened before,' Ignacio the driver said – the huge empty *meseta* began, the air grew clear and sharp and the sun drove the whorls of mist away. At Castromonte we left the highroad and drove mile upon mile past *fincas* and *haciendas*, broad and sweeping as western ranches, their boundaries marked by lines of trees, sparkling with frost. Now and then we passed a countryman riding a mule, his head wrapped in a blanket against the cold with one eye peeping out, like an Arab woman's: otherwise there was no one and nothing but the enormous white expanse of country and absolute peace.

That is to say, there would have been absolute peace but for Ignacio. He was young and loquacious and, unlike most of his colleagues, bubbling over with zest. For the first part of our drive he extolled the beauties of Valladolid, past, present and to come; and now, the beauties of nature lost upon him, he turned predictably to the bull-fight and its maestros, whose varying techniques he discussed with great authority, in particular those of el Cordobés.

'You must have seen him often,' I observed. The cult for that crude, if valiant, showman had always mystified me, but perhaps appreciation came with time.

'Once, just once,' Ignacio replied, 'but I shall never forget it.' He paused for a moment, dreamily smiling. 'He was in his white Mercedes, at Valladolid, oh, near as near. I could have put out my hand and touched him. I saw the Mercedes coming: I looked at the number: and it was he! For I had read of his *coche* in the papers. They gave the matricula, and I had memorized it. As he approached, my heart seemed to fly into my mouth. Then, he was gone. Everyone was cheering and clapping. All over in a moment, Señora, yet such a moment is like a great piece of life.'

He drove on, sunk in a reverie, and I was respectfully silent. All at once he braked, with such force that I was thrown against the windscreen.

'Look!' he cried, pointing out a hare that capered across a field, while I dabbed the blood from my nose. 'It is very auspicious to see a hare, and very unusual at this time of year.' The hare and the luck it would bring us kept him in talk until we reached La Espina.

The Thorn, from which this fourteenth-century Cistercian monastery took its name, was said of course to have come from the Saviour's crown; and the title, Countess of the Holy Thorn, was at one time conceded to a local Marquesa, an honour as great as elegant, and surely unsurpassed by the Golden Rose itself. And the looks of the place promised well, with its massive church and twin towers stately beside the ample harmonious buildings of the community. What no one, least of all my black-hearted guidebook, had thought to mention was, that it had now become a training college for *capataces*, or foremen, under the auspices of the Ministry for Agriculture. Fleeing *desarrollo* in Valladolid, I had driven all this distance to encounter it here.

Ignacio rushed at the front door bell and rang it until an attendant appeared, with inquiry and disapproval in his face, as if bells were not for ringing. On hearing that this foreign lady, herself a farmer, was anxious to see the school and its up-to-date methods – Ignacio was fond of the word up-to-date – he relaxed and nodded benignly, as if such pilgrims were common. We were handed over to one of the students, a grave unsmiling boy, who escorted us through the entire establishment, classrooms, lecture-halls, the refectory, dormitories, bathrooms, as well as barns, sheds and stables outside. He spoke hardly at all, and then with an air of quotation: there were, he said, 150 pupils here, in this 'ambiente digno, confortable y austero', receiving their 'formación' as useful citizens and cultivators. The word 'formation', by the way, is constantly used now instead of 'education', which seems to imply a change of outlook as much as of vocabulary. Everything we saw was excellently kept and in plain good Spanish taste; but the atmosphere of the house was anything but Spanish, reminiscent indeed of countries behind the Iron Curtain. The boys' commonroom was adorned with technical pictures and diagrams, and printed slogans such as Do Not Toil Alone! United We Triumph, Divided We Fall! Cooperation Means Progress! and other expressions of alien sentiment. Everything new in Spain at present is copied from abroad, and here it looked as if the authorities, poring over some contraband

Red publication, had picked up a few helpful ideas.

Ignacio was entranced with it all and continually pointed out how up-to-date everything was, including a herd of Hereford cows and a sty full of Large White pigs. Over and over again he inquired if similar places existed in England, and was delighted to hear that at least I knew of none. One thing led to another, and on the homeward drive, he fairly put me through it: had we television, telephones, skyscrapers, lifts, aeroplanes? or a Metro, like the one in Madrid? I claimed them all but the sky-scrapers, but he did not seem to be wholly convinced.

'At any rate you have the Queen,' he said, gracefully changing the subject. Next he treated me to some of those astonishing facts of Royal life which one has to go to the Continent to hear. At Castromonte, he decided as an additional treat for me, that we would visit the mineral water bottling factory there. I demurred, having hoped to make up for the disappointment of La Espina by looking in at Tordesillas, but Ignacio was not to be deflected.

'There is nothing at Tordesillas,' he assured me.

Nor there was, from his point of view, nothing but ghosts and relics, the great convent of Sta Clara overlooking the river Duero, with the room where Joan the Mad, mother of Charles V, spent her last forty-nine years, mopping and mowing for her dead but worthless husband, or strumming on one of her three clavichords, Flemish, Spanish and Arab, all intact and more or less in tune, and the coffer in which Isabel of Portugal shut a beautiful maid of honour for three days and three nights, the girl surviving miraculously to become a nun, and the dining hall where Napoleon supped with the Abbess, who ought to have poisoned him, and historical documents beautifully prepared by scribes and signed with a kingly scrawl, ancient books, Arab works of art, a lovely Mudejar patio with the original pillars and arches and a pattern of fig leaves and pine cones, cunningly arabicized, over the walls, and the church with its carvings, tombs and portraits of the great and holy.

One of these was of San Pedro Regalado, showing a bull

about to attack him and falling dead in the nick of time, a miracle which raised him to glory as patron of *toreros*. I tried him on Ignacio as an inducement, but without avail: evidently, for one who had seen el Cordobés close to in his white Mercedes, San Pedro Regalado was pretty small beer. And so we went to see the springs and the bottling-rooms, with their shiny machines and contented women workers, tubes, wheels and vats, forests of empty bottles in the yard outside, the *administrador* in spotless white, everything neat as a new pin. And it was like that every day, Ignacio emphasized, for no one had expected our coming. I learned that fizzy mineral water does not gush from the earth a-bubble but is *bicarbonada* after drawing, and many more facts of equal fascination: indeed, I left the place knowing all there was to know on this riveting subject, and, almost at once, completely forgot it again.

As we sped down the *carretera* towards the city, Ignacio in full spate, an extraordinary thing occurred. A covered waggon, drawn by a pair of mules, was moving slowly in our direction: it was keeping its side of the road, we ours, and yet, in passing, Ignacio managed to overturn it. It was not the event itself that was extraordinary, although sufficiently bizarre, but the fact of my having somehow foreknown it. The moment I clapped eyes on that waggon I knew, in a flash of clairvoyance, that we were set for collision. Nor did my psychic intuitions stop at that. I next realized, perhaps deep down had realized all along, that Ignacio was not a genuine cabby, that it was not his car and that he had no business driving it. How this could be was a puzzle, for the arrangements had been made by the hotel, who dealt only with one firm, connected with this by marriage; but such I now knew in my bones was the case.

Having got the mules to their feet, the owner berated Ignacio at the top of his lungs, while the culprit stood gloomily by, speechless at last. Again I had a peculiar psychic sense, this time of having lived through the whole she-mozzle before, step by step. A *guardia* on a motorbicycle drew up and began to make inquiries. One after another, the cards went down on the table. Ignacio had no driving-licence, the car was insured but not he. The owner was his cousin and, taken suddenly ill, had deputed him to make his apologies to the hotel and to the Señora; but he had hit on what seemed to him a more constructive and fruitful plan. Notifying his employer, who was in the haberdashery line, that he would not be available that morning, he had stood in for his cousin, to maintain the family interest and spare the Señora the *molestia* of looking for alternative transport.

None of this moving confession touched the *guardia* in the slightest. Policeman to the marrow, he was all bogged down in a technical swamp of licences and insurance. Having taken copious notes, he put his book away, helped us all to set the waggon on its wheels and, leaving his motor bicycle on the bank, signified that he was ready to drive us home. Not another word was spoken, the whole way there. On the back seat crouched Ignacio, head in hands. First, I was dropped at my hotel.

'What do I owe you, don Ignacio?' I asked, with the grave courtesy due to the fallen.

A despairing shake of the head was the only response.

'Then tell your cousin to see me about it,' I suggested.

Ignacio looked up in horror. 'I will never dare go near him again,' he mumbled. 'This car is his niño.' And in truth the *niño* had suffered more by way of dents and scratches than the sturdy old waggon itself.

A saying of an Austrian friend came into my mind, and I passed it on: 'You know, very often a bad experience makes a good memory.'

If he saw a gleam of hope in this, he gave no sign of it. As I mounted the hotel steps the car drove on, whither, I could but fearfully surmise. And I prayed that the hare we had seen that morning would come up to scratch: I must confess that, to me, it had looked almost as zany as Ignacio himself.

17

Whether it was the hare, the Espina, or the mineral water factory, I woke next morning with a high fever and was out of action for some three weeks. After that, there was a longish piece of research to do in the archives at Simancas, so that spring was on the way before I got back to Madrid. But now I was there, and best of all had found room in the Hotel Paris. That is something no longer to count on, a new feature of Spanish life being the itinerant *grupo*, or likeminded persons travelling about in a bunch and crowding the individual out. And the *ambiente* itself had undergone changes since first I knew it, thirty-odd years ago. This had to be expected, especially as even then it was a good half-century behind the times. It would have been the ideal setting for a novel by Galdós, for scenes perhaps from *Fortunato y Jacinta*, that welter of middle-class madrileño life which, miraculously for so fecund an author, he compressed into seventeen hundred pages.

The best parlour was always locked unless a lady felt disposed to 'tocar' the piano there. When this happened, a young man with curly side whiskers would gravely open the door, entrusting her with the key for locking up again at the end of her recital. Chandeliers were rife, immense and glittering in the *salas públicas*, modest in passageway or bedroom, but all curiously lopsided where the crystals had fallen off, like fruit from a tree. There was an abundance of heavy white lace, crimson plush and velvet, and gold-leaf paint. The beds were massive four-posters, with looped curtains and stout wooden legs, on which flowers were painted by what seemed to be an amateur brush. The bathrooms were princely, the floor an expanse of gleaming if chilly marble, a rusted iron bath under the chandelier in the middle and all around a complex of water-pipes, now emitting a strangled moan, now breaking into a roar, but seldom wholly at peace.

Much, nearly all, of this had gradually disappeared. New lifts had been installed, so that people no longer walked upstairs if pressed for time. The plumbing today was capricious rather than totally insane. The small pages in smart livery and silver buttons, dashing here and there on every conceivable errand, had given place to youths in slacks and pullovers, who apparently had little inclination to move at all. The dining-room had lost its chandelier and with it its agreeable atmosphere, both formal and festive. Now it was lit by rows of round expressionless lamps, set rigidly nautical-fashion in the ceiling, as if the room were liable to be rocked by forty-foot waves.

But despite these changes, and the encroachment of a new sort of clientèle, it remains as it always was, pleasant, easy and reassuring. This happy state of affairs is probably thanks to a nucleus of the staff having been there all along, for it is amazing, almost magical, how just a few old-timers can hold a place together. Henry James once wrote, with his eye on a butler, of the peculiar dignity a man acquires by spending his life in the one house and daily performing the one round of duties, and this is well illustrated here. The concierge knows Madrid from end to end and inside out, unlike almost every policeman: he is also up in all that is going on, which *atracciones* must be seen and which are merely *regular:* he remembers every client and his odd little fancies; and, except that he now wears spectacles for reading, seems not to have changed a whit in thirty years. The senior waiters too are their old familiar selves, spick and span, dignified, courteous and patient, like Elder Statesmen. There may be a tinge of melancholy in their faces when *grupos* arrive, with the noisy chatter, demands and complaints by which 'new' people hope to make their presence felt, but there is no departure from standards or adjustments to levels not their own. Lavish spending impresses them not in the least. One of the pleasantest things I saw was the *mayor domo* break off in the act of taking some expensive order to greet an elderly couple, long known to him, escort them to their table and settle them in, ask how they were, find out what they wanted and then, with his own hands, reverently place before them a bottle containing an inch of wine, left from their previous meal. I could happily have stayed there for months, but my illness had thrown things out and soon I should have to take my leave.

Shortly after my arrival, a legal friend invited me to pay a visit to the Labour Court, where he was employed, and I was very glad to do so, having no firsthand experience of any Spanish courts at all. The lawyers were dressed in long black open robes, somewhat like a dressing-gown, with a brief squared cape or pelerin round the shoulders. Some were of plain material, some of velvet, which probably corresponded to our stuff and silk. As most of them were short and fat, they looked like pursy little housekeepers in a clerical institution.

The proceedings themselves were very different from what I had expected. I was of course aware that the exploited, bullied, defenceless Spanish worker was a figment of foreign socialist fancy; but I had also heard much of the dilatory ways of Spanish tribunals and the labyrinths of red tape that snarled them up. Here at any rate, causes were dealt with in a brisk and sensible fashion, no one sending out for musty legal tomes to peer at and every counsel alert, with the facts at his fingertips. Interesting too was the modesty of the claims being argued. A dispute involving the equivalent of ten or fifteen pounds would take up an hour or more, numerous witnesses being called, and even recalled, to go over some point again. Unless Spanish lawyers plead for the simple joy of hearing their tongues go clack, costs must greatly exceed the amount at issue. Of the awe which surrounds the judiciary in England, there was not a trace. Everyone spoke up freely, in or out of turn. At one moment a *magistrado*, two counsels and a workman were all vociferating together, and peace only fell when the *magistrado* suddenly banged on his desk and bawled, in good Andaluz, 'but we are all saying the same thing!'

Outside, the vestibule was crowded with litigants and their lawyers, all feverishly smoking and throwing their butts on the floor while they gave each other last-minute advice. A footman walked round and round, sweeping the debris up, which apparently was his life work. It was in chatting here to a young *abogado*, while I waited for the next case in which don Luis was to plead, that I learned of the suit pending against Manuel Summers, which I have referred to earlier on. Last September, five of his cartoons had appeared in the *Sábado Gráfico*, one of the livelier weeklies, creating a wonderful stir among the *bien-pensants* and leading to a charge of *escarnio contra la religion católica*.

Summers' drawings were familiar to me, as always amusing, often mischievous, not invariably in the finest of taste, but never outrageous. I could not imagine work from his pen that any rational being would consider as such. The thing to do, clearly, was to have a look at them, which sounds a good deal simpler than it turned out to be. The editor of the *Sábado Gráfico* was sorry, but the police had carried every last copy away. At the Palacio de Justicia, where the case was down for trial, no one knew anything about it and appeared, reasonably enough, to think it no business of mine. I next tried the British Embassy, which recommended a Reading Room where files of all the periodicals were kept. (Incidentally, the man I saw spoke no English and sent me to the wrong address; but the *hispanización* of our Embassy is another story.) In time I found it, and was given a form, which I then had to take back to the Embassy for endorsement. By now I had travelled some thirty-five miles. Back to the Reading Room, to be sent off again to procure three photographs: this done, I waited while a young woman sulkily copied the *tarjeta* of admission three times over and demanded four pesetas. I had only a five-peseta piece, and she had no change, nor would she hear of keeping the extra one: it must be four single pesetas or nothing. At last the man behind me in the now lengthening queue paid up, and the young woman relaxed.

'Ahora puede pasar,' she said, all smiles, handing me one copy and retaining the others for God knew what.

The superintendent of the Reading Room examined the card severely, conceded that it was in order, asked what I wanted and, brightening, said that almost certainly they had not got it, which proved after forty minutes or so to be the case. But there was a similar Room he said, only miles and miles away in San Augustín. By now I had worked myself into the frame of mind, single and bloody, of Victor Hugo's detective Javert, and I would have gone many times as far and knocked on a whole new series of doors. But in Spain the last thing you expect is what often happens. At San Augustín, in a spotless comfortable *sala de lectura*, empty but for the man in charge and myself, the famous cartoons were produced in a matter of minutes.

So this was what I had combed Madrid to see! I could hardly believe my eyes. There was a group of bishops and priests noisily debating celibacy, while an old woman in the flat below banged with a broom on the ceiling for quiet. At a sort of box office by the door of a church, a priest accompanied by a woman was saying, 'Give me two reclinatorios in the second row.' A *reclinatorio* can be either a stool to kneel on at prayer, or a couch; but since he was taking two of them, the innuendo seemed fairly mild. A man kneeling at confession fumbles in his pockets, while the priest says 'That makes 345.70 . . . and whatever you like (y la voluntad).' A corpulent friar grins and rubs his hands while a pretty girl (Spain) coyly murmurs in his ear, 'Ah, Father 'Ultra', that's what you tell them all.'

The drawings were decidedly anticlerical in tone, but the charge was of ridiculing, or scoffing at (*escarnio*) the

Catholic religion itself, not the clergy. The prosecution further alleged that they 'materialized the spiritual', whatever that might mean. At the subsequent hearing, which was in camera, two priests appeared for the defence and denied that the cartoons were injurious to the faith. One of them was secretary to the Archbishop of Madrid, the other a distinguished theologian, but their evidence was ignored and the artist condemned. Quite likely the outcome was determined in advance by higher authority, and the court held as a matter of form, in the traditional way. In some respects at least, Spain had hardly changed at all.

By now the day was gone. I walked back to the hotel in beautiful evening light, San Jerónimo clear and sharp against the sky. Guarding the entrance to the Cortes were the two proud lions, imperial paw on globe, cast from cannon seized in the Moroccan war of 1860 after a heroic action by General Prim. Inside nowadays there gathers a docile flock, orating, applauding, jumping through the hoops in fervent make-believe. No one here was going to table a motion, 'That this House deplores the treatment of the artist Summers.' No one here was ever going to throw down a challenge of any kind whatever. There is a story of a visiting potentate who looked at one of the elaborate bridges over the Manzanares and thoughtfully observed, 'They should either sell that bridge or buy a river.' And tonight I had a similar feeling about the lions and the Cortes. One or the other should really go: the conjunction, today, is absurd.

Meanwhile, matters of far greater importance were looming up. The Caudillo's granddaughter was to marry Alfonso de Borbón. It was hardly a case of 'in robe and crown, the king stepped down', the bride's father being the Marqués de Villaverde and Sra Franco reputedly one of the richest women in Spain; but public opinion, as far as there was any, seemed to be that the Francos had fully and finally got there. No one took very much interest in it, and what private comment I heard was cynical; but there was a great to-do in the press, the bride's beauty, the groom's manly charm, the trousseau, the list of those invited, the splendour and luxury of the arrangements, and the plans for the honeymoon, being gone into thoroughly.

In true Spanish style, the pedigrees of all concerned were given right back to the mists of time. And there was a peculiar fascination in that of the Caudillo himself. The eminent scholar don Julio Caro Baroja affirms in his book on the Jews of Spain *Los Judíos en la España moderna y contemporanea*, 1961, that the Francos were of that race. Now it appeared that they were of most noble, most ancient French stock, having come to Spain 'en época muy remota' to help fight the Moors, going from glory to glory and culminating at last in don Francisco Franco y Bahamonde. This revelation somehow put me in mind of that exquisite moment in Lampedusa's *Leopard*, when don Calogero Sedàra the parvenu mayor, having itemized the magnificent dowry his daughter would bring Salina's nephew (a dowry mostly filched from Salina himself) concludes: 'And Prince . . . the Sedàra are noble too; till I came along we've been an unlucky lot, buried in the provinces and undistinguished, but I have the documents in order, and one day it will be known that your nephew has married the Baronessina Sedàra del Biscotto . . . ' The Prince neither knew nor cared if this were true, any more than I could judge between don Julio and the doubtless able genealogist; but he had 'the incomparable artistic satisfaction of seeing a type realized in all its details,' and in that satisfaction, at least, I was able to share.

It seemed curiously out of date in any event, this clinging to *hidalguía* while the country grows ever more urban and proletarian. But the regime altogether is anachronistic, still thinking in terms of the twenties and thirties, still trouncing democracy and boosting dictatorship, still painting up Franco! Franco! Franco! on the walls and more then ever convinced that Spain is a model to the rest of the world. It even continues to reward prolific parents, in the style of Mussolini: only the other day a man of 107 was *premiado* for his contribution to the world's overcrowding. As for the externals, the suits and trappings, they are sheer Ruritania. At the Pardo, where the Caudillo resides, the streets fairly swarm with military who appear to have no function beyond that of harassing visitors. Whichever way you turn, you fetch up against some officer, spick and span and extremely polite, who nevertheless waves you back. By spick and span, I mean wearing a smart uniform with plenty of crimson braid: he is almost sure to be gloveless, smoking, and carrying a suitcase or brown paper parcel. Every fifty yards or so stands an armed sentry, with *no pasarán!* written all over him, although no one dreams of attempting to do so. Through a gateway in the courtyard of the palace itself I got a glimpse of two Moorish bodyguards, those romantic figures that used to ride through the capital on state occasions, lance in hand, helmet swathed in flowing turban, mounted on fiery horses whose hooves were painted gold. They never appear in public now and I stopped to admire them; but even a moment's pause was not allowed and a soldier hastily shoo'd me away.

The little old town itself was always charming, with a feel of Austria in the trim lanes and honey-coloured houses, and it was more than ever attractive today with the rows of almond and plum in early flower. But in the very heart of it, right before the palace gate, was a cluster of new shops selling frightful souvenirs, kiosks for postcard – though none of the Pardo, which is sacrosanct – more *viviendas*, taverns and restaurants done up in the *cursi* style of the day. On a grass verge I saw a number of people, mostly nuns and schoolchildren, standing in a ring and chortling away at something or other. The cause of their mirth proved to be a fountain, in which was the figure of a chubby little boy with water spouting from his penis, a replica perhaps of that Mannekenpiss of Brussels which appears to have taken the Spanish fancy.

All these things were ignoble enough, considered one by one, and viewed as a whole they formed a tableau vivant of Franco's Spain. The words about Christopher Wren in St

Paul's fit the case very nicely; and if the Caudillo should himself seek his monument, he has merely to glance through the window.

Meanwhile, for it was Sunday, coaches were pulling in and depositing numbers of petits-bourgeois, all men, all middle-aged and all with cameras slung round their necks. They were merrier and noisier than such people used to be, and also fatter: this generation puts on inches as fast as the young nowadays but, theirs being outward rather than upward bound, it only makes them seem the more a different race. I wondered how so larky a lot came to be here and whether they might not tangle with the military; but it soon turned out that they were *grupos*, each under the iron discipline of a leader, to be marched hither and yon to the few historic places open to the public, instructed, fed and carried off again. As soon as the coaches were empty, the laughing and joking abruptly died, like the sound track in a Spanish film: docile as raw recruits, the *grupos* fell in and moved off, myself looking on open-mouthed, half expecting them to break into the goose-step or sing 'Die Fahne hoch, the Reihen dicht geschlossen.'

This was to be my last day in Spain, and the experiences so far were depressing. To comfort myself I went to visit the Cristo de el Pardo, a splendid work of Gregorio Hernández in the Capucine church. The way led over a river and up a steepish hill, with a lovely view of the Sierras, capped with snow, and flowering shrubs on every side. Merely to leave the town and cross the bridge, with the full green waters rushing and gurgling below, brought back a sense of calm and peace; but it was not for long. All too soon I came on a military band, hard at work rehearsing, playing a single dire phrase over and over. The brass produced such screams as only Spanish bugles or terrified pigs can, while the drums were quite extraordinary, unable, as it appeared, to agree among themselves. Some held to a steady normal beat, others favoured the wild tacky rhythm of a *zapateado*, resulting in a diabolical point counterpoint that only a dervish could possibly march to.

178

'Better, but still not perfect,' the conductor said, at the conclusion of every try. 'Once again!'

Their strivings after perfection followed me up for another half mile or so. By then I had reached what looked to be a grand estate, protected by tall iron railings and the notice, Patrimonio Nacional: Prohibida la Entrada. A man in the brown corduroys and wide hat of a park-keeper stood at the gate and, as I went towards him, immediately started waving his arms like all the others until I began to think that everyone here was suffering from St Vitus dance.

'I only wanted to ask what this Patrimonio Nacional might be,' I assured him.

'Why do you wish to know?' he countered, with much severity in his look.

I was simply curious as to why, if it was Patrimonio Nacional, no one was allowed in; but information for information's sake is what no Spaniard ever looks for or believes that anyone else does, nor does he welcome direct inquiry.

'Just because it looks so pretty and nicely kept.'

'Aha!' He was instantly mollified. 'It is a golf course. The golf course of the Caudillo.'

'Indeed! Does he use it much?' For the Generalísimo's golfing days must surely have drawn to a close.

'Never.'

The reply came with a quiet authority, a full conviction as to its sense and logic, that the Mad Hatter himself could barely have surpassed. Enhancing the Wonderland touch, at that very moment two mounted police galloped over the green towards us, reined in and stiffly saluted.

'Qué pasa?'

'Nada.'

'Everything in order?'

'Everything in order.'

And with another stiff salute the pair of them galloped away.

Musing, I went on up the hill and presently came to the church. Outside a knot of young people, bawling transistors in hand, were drinking holy water from a tap set in the wall. It was in an alcove, with wrought-iron lanterns on either side and a background of tiles bearing quotations from St Francis about Sister Earth and Sister Water, in the kind of script used for facetious mottoes in public houses. Evidently the good fathers had been up to the same tricks as everyone else. In time, no doubt, funds permitting, the scene will be further embellished with plaster figures of Sister Rabbit and Brother Frog.

But within the church there was utter peace. Boxes of tools, shrouded pictures and a carpet of dust revealed that here, too, *obras* were in hand; but it was Sunday and the workmen were at home. A solitary monk knelt at the feet of the Cristo, recumbent on his elevated bier. Otherwise the building was empty, the morning Masses all being said.

It is difficult to describe the marvel wrought by Hernández in this Christ Crucified. There is all the agony of death in the broken body, the yawning wounds and caking blood, the sightless half-shut eyes, the mouth twisted in pain, the thorn-pierced brow. Good Spaniard that he was, the artist spares us nothing. The human anguish is faithfully, cruelly, mercilessly shown. But, in some miraculous way, it is seen as irrelevant. The whole figure radiates the serenity of spiritual triumph, annihilating the body's humiliation. How the wonder was achieved is beyond my power of analysis. Some Kunsthistoriker could perhaps explain it all in erudite fashion, how this line effected that, that curve this, these masses, those planes, the balance here, the emphasis there, *Einheit von Begriff und Auswirkung* . . . I should be none the wiser, and probably less. Magic is more to my taste than science, reverence than expertise. Here was abject death and glorious life, co-existent, brought into being by the artist's hand from the lump of inanimate matter before him; and for me, it was enough.

And so the last day in Spain was sweetened after all, sweetened by voices from the past, but no matter. In the afternoon I went a long walk by the river banks and into the country, beyond the zone of *entradas prohibidas,* along sandy paths and through woods of umbrella pine. Now and then I met a stag, rubbing his antlers against a tree, or a doe with her fawn. They looked at me calmly, showing no fear and never moving as I passed, as if people seldom disturbed them. They and the birds were all the living creatures I came across. The Sunday sportsmen that abound almost everywhere, loosing off barrel after barrel, were notably absent, banned from the area perhaps by way of precaution: although there was no need for this, anything or anyone they aimed at being perfectly secure.

Then as evening fell I returned to the Pardo, to get the coach for Madrid. Somewhere or other, I had dropped my little leather purse for holding coins, and went into a boutique to buy another. It was very pretty, made of soft elephant hide with the *escudo* of Madrid embossed in silver on one side; and it was also far from cheap, in fact quite up to top European level. This led, as I waited for the bus, to dismal thoughts of the Whither Spain? description. Was she to become, as apparently she intended, just one more efficient, competitive, inflationary centre of production? Turning out goods and more goods, capturing markets? I feared so. The coach arrived, I got in, the conductor asked for my fare, I took out my smart little purse and opened it. It promptly fell to pieces, quite to pieces, the framework came away in my hand, the *escudo* and the money dropped to the floor; and as I stooped to gather them up, my heart was filled with joy and relief.